"Kathy Escobar is a fearless, joy[
living in both stories and systen
in. *Turning Over Tables* reminc
that our personal transformation is ...
and that faith should and can be a catalyst for both. The path to
individual and shared renovation is perilous, but Escobar shows us
why the beauty we might experience is so worth the grieving and
the growing necessary to reveal it."
—John Pavlovitz, author of *Worth Fighting For*
and *If God Is Love, Don't Be a Jerk*

"Escobar is a consistent voice of humility, honesty, and hope.
Prophetic, timely, and wise, this book will challenge you in all
the best ways and lead to transformation."
—Sarah Bessey, author of *A Rhythm of Prayer*
and *Field Notes for the Wilderness*

"We Christians often refer to God as 'the Almighty,' and sadly,
we often make ourselves in that image, acting as if power (for our
ego, our gender, our denomination, our party, or our nation) is
something to be grasped, amassed, and hoarded. That's why I'm
so grateful that Kathy Escobar invites us to devote the season
of Lent to a time of reflection on power. Get ready though . . .
because this well-written book is powerful enough to challenge
your assumptions about power!"
—Brian D. McLaren, author of *Life after Doom*

"Many Christians know the image of a gentle and peaceful Jesus,
but few have truly encountered the Jesus who boldly challenged
systems of power, flipped tables, and demanded justice for the
poor, oppressed, and marginalized. In this compelling and deeply
pastoral devotional, Kathy Escobar invites us to walk alongside
this radical Jesus—the one who not only taught but embodied
the vision of a more just and equal world. This resource is both
inspiring and challenging, offering Christians a transformative
guide to aligning their lives with the way of Jesus, especially on
the Lenten journey."
—Brandan Robertson, author of *Queer
& Christian* and *Filled to Be Emptied*

"*Turning Over Tables* is a capacious invitation to discover afresh the liberative, healing, and empire-subverting way of Jesus. Drawing deeply from her own journey with love and justice, Kathy Escobar awakens us to see that every time Jesus pointed to the kin-dom of God, Jesus was flipping the tables of oppression and power abuse. This is a book to read, share, and practice with a handful of others also gripped by Jesus' imagination of shalom for all and everything."

—Dwight J. Friesen, Professor of Practical Theology at The Seattle School of Theology & Psychology and author of *2020s Foresight* (coauthored with Tom Sine) and *The New Parish*

"The power of Lent may best be realized in exploring power itself! Kathy Escobar helps us examine and critique the forms of power we wield. Using accessible and insightful prose, Escobar's work will help both individuals and groups turn over tables for good. And what better time to consider power than in a season that proclaims the power of love!"

—Thomas Jay Oord, author of *The Death of Omnipotence and Birth of Amipotence*

"Conversations about power can be tricky. We might ignore it because it's too uncomfortable or exaggerate Jesus' flipping of tables to justify our own spurious outbursts. Thankfully, Kathy Escobar has the experience and the insight to be a faithful and wise guide in this arena. Her latest book takes us where we may not want to go, but go we must, for too much is at stake."

—Colby Martin, author of *The Shift* and *UnClobber*

Turning Over Tables

Access free digital resources, which include a sermon series guide, videos for group study from the author, images for use during worship or group study, and resources to promote your outreach, at www.wjkbooks.com/TurningOverTables.

Turning Over Tables

A Lenten Call for Disrupting Power

Kathy Escobar

WESTMINSTER
JOHN KNOX PRESS
LOUISVILLE · KENTUCKY

First edition
Published by Westminster John Knox Press
Louisville, Kentucky

25 26 27 28 29 30 31 32 33 34—10 9 8 7 6 5 4 3 2 1

Book design by Drew Stevens
Cover design by Luisa Dias

Library of Congress Cataloging-in-Publication Data is on file at the Library of Congress, Washington, DC.

ISBN: 978-0-664-26831-2 (paperback)
ISBN: 978-1-646-98411-4 (ebook)

Contents

Introduction

ENTER

"Enter through the narrow gate, for the gate is wide and the road is easy that leads to destruction, and there are many who take it. For the gate is narrow and the road is hard that leads to life, and there are few who find it."
—Matthew 7:13–14

Many years ago, I worked at a megachurch as an adult ministry pastor and had an experience some of you might be able to relate to personally, or perhaps you've seen it happen to others. While I loved my job and being in the trenches with people cultivating opportunities for transformation in community, I quickly realized the system I was serving was extremely unhealthy. Women in leadership were less-than, scapegoating people was normal, pretty and financially resourced people were clearly valued the most, and a focus on being the biggest and best church around was the driving force for all decisions.

My awakening felt like what happened in the apostle Paul's conversion and healing from blindness: "And immediately something like scales fell from his eyes, and his sight was restored. Then he got up and was baptized, and after taking some food, he regained his strength" (Acts 9:18–19).

When my eyes were finally opened to the overt and covert realities of unhealthy power in a system built on the name of Jesus, something shifted in the deepest part of my soul and experience. It was not a clean and easy transition. It was brutal, painful, and disorienting. When I began calling out unhealthy power, showing up at elder meetings and asking them to consider their power and to use it on behalf of the least and the last, they shifted in their seats a little and patted me on the head, chalking up my comments to naiveté because they were all older, wiser, and more seasoned. Then, as I got increasingly vocal and stronger and rocked the boat more openly, I quickly found myself out of leadership, out of the church, and out of all I once had given my whole heart to. I didn't just lose my job in the process; I also lost a big part of who I was as a Christian.

Initially, it was one of the worst things that ever happened to me. Now I consider it a gift. Seeing the cycle of misused power in the name of God up close and personal helped me come back to why I started following Jesus in the first place—his wild and countercultural ways of disrupting existing power structures and caring for the most marginalized in society.

Almost every single Jesus story—from his birth to death to resurrection—reveals an inversion of the world's understanding of power. He touched lepers and dined with sinners. He turned over tables and called out religiosity on its hypocrisy. He told everybody that they needed to be last, not first. He said that love transcended all, that the way toward God was not up but down to the places of real life, real pain, and that God desired mercy, not sacrifice.

When my "sight was restored" and my eyes were opened to the ravages of unhealthy power, my heart was emboldened with hope for a better way. I was baptized into a new season of life, emerging far more passionate about disrupting toxic power; cultivating equity, activism, and systems change; and embodying the wild ways of Jesus collectively. For the past two decades since then, I have been working alongside people on the margins of life and faith and continue to see how power dynamics are at play in almost every system and circumstance. How we feel about ourselves in relationship to others, how we treat people different from us, who gets to lead and make decisions, who influences systems that affect us, and what impacts are felt from being on the underside of unhealthy power and oppressive systems are always running in a strong undercurrent in our groups, systems, and society.

However, I've continued to find that in most social circles power isn't the most popular topic. Why is it so hard to talk about? I think it's because power can feel invisible to us even though it is tied to almost every aspect of our lives. Especially for white, privileged, and resourced people of faith like me—and maybe like you—power is not something we readily notice. It's a lot like an iceberg—we see only its tip, but a massive mass exists underneath. Jim Henderson, a writer, speaker, and faith-conversation pot stirrer, once shared these simple words at a conference that I'll never forget: "People with power never think about it, and people without power think about it all of the time."[1]

But what is power, really? And why is it so important to engage with as people of faith? Most definitions of power include something along the lines of the ability to control or have influence over others. In its simplest form, I think power is the ability to influence and catalyze through position, value, voice, and resources.

The ability to influence and catalyze through position, value, voice, and resources.

Reverend Dr. Martin Luther King Jr. said that "Power, properly understood, is the ability to achieve purpose. It is the strength required to bring about social, political, or economic changes."[2] Dr. Cedar Barstow, founder of the Right Use of Power Institute, defines power as "the ability to have an effect or have influence."[3] Jesus never specifically defined power, but he used stories and embodiment to flesh out a totally contradictory form of power than the traditional system.

Power is always at play as one of the most core realities in all social systems, faith-based or not. The Right Use of Power Institute expounds five types of power that are bedrock to conversations about power:

1. Personal power is "each individual's ability to have an effect or influence."
2. Role or Positional power is "earned, awarded, elected, or assigned" like a vocational position, family role, or specific job.

3. Status power is additional power that is added to us by the cultures we're in and can include "race, age, ability, gender, and socioeconomics."
4. Collective power comes from "gathering personal, role, and status power from multiple sources to effect change toward a common interest."
5. Systemic power is "centered on the combined efforts of collective power that shifts systems, structures, laws, policies, and norms."[4]

We're not going to deep dive into these different forms of power, but they're important to tuck into our heads and hearts as we travel through this material together. It's crucial that we recognize we all have power. Power, in and of itself, isn't bad or negative; *it is what we choose to do with that power that matters.* Unhealthy power is centered on control and diminishing others while healthy power catalyzes liberation and life. Disempowerment—whether it stems from institutions, cultures, or families—limits and harms, while empowerment frees and heals. Popular author, speaker, and researcher Brené Brown writes and speaks extensively about the difference between power over and power with/to/within, especially in leadership and relationship. In the briefest summary, power over is centered on fear, hierarchy, scarcity, and being right, while power with/to/within is built on empathy, expansion, and connection.[5]

Jesus embodied power built on empathy, expansion, and connection, not fear, hierarchy and scarcity. He called his followers to a completely different kind of relationship with power that would bring a new kind of kingdom on earth, here, now. Sadly, Christians aren't leading the way in this conversation on power. We lag behind, and we're some of the worst examples of unhealthy power. Colonization, patriarchy, racism, classism, ableism, and the lies of white supremacy and Christian supremacy are all intensely embedded into our story in the world. And I'm not talking just about Christian history and past sins; I'm talking about today. Here, now. These dysfunctional beliefs and practices are baked into American Christianity and affect and guide us in ways in which we are often unaware.

While Jesus' words in the Beatitudes about spiritual poverty, mourning, meekness, mercy, justice, and peacemaking were about turning the world upside down, we continue to do all we can to turn it right side up. In other words—our side up.

While Jesus embodied a life of descent, going down into the depths of real problems and pain, so much of the world and often the church is dedicated to the principles of ascent. Instead of caring for the vulnerable, it's often about survival of the fittest. Instead of toppling oppressive systems, most of the energy is spent on preserving and protecting them. Instead of a dedication to equity and sharing, hierarchy and hoarding still prevail.

The deeper I have dived into conversations and practices centered on healthy power, the more I realize I have only scratched the surface.

The roots of unhealthy power run deep.

Our need to stay in control and on top is strong, even primal.

Our addiction to comfort, charismatic leaders, and hierarchical leadership is astonishingly predictable.

Our ineptitude at vulnerable self-reflection and honest conversations about power is extremely disturbing.

For those who are part of families and systems that have diminished or abused us, our inability to own our personal power and God's image in us is heartbreaking.

And for individuals and groups oppressed by dominant power systems, the lack of a willingness by those systems to humbly address and boldly shift power is destructive.

Even though we rarely address it directly, power dynamics are baked into all areas of our lives, including personal and social dynamics, politics, religion, and our relationship with ourselves and others. Power influences our behavior and interactions and overtly and covertly shapes relationships, decision-making processes, and ways in which resources and opportunities in our communities are distributed.

We can't transform ourselves, our communities, or the world without honestly and bravely engaging in conversations and reflections that challenge our personal relationship to power and how that plays out in the circles in which we live and move. How is our unawareness of our personal power limiting us? How are we complicit in unhealthy power structures? How have we been harmed by power? How have we harmed others? How have we given our power to people and systems who used it to amass more for themselves? How is our lack of self-reflection about the power we hold affecting others? How can we play a part in turning over tables and disrupt systems that are unjust and oppressive? These are the kinds of things we need to address more directly in order to cultivate healthy power in our broken world.

To me, the season of Lent, on the road to Easter, is always about intentionally opening ourselves up to what's underneath the surface, what's hidden in the dark, what tectonic plates need to shift for something new to be born. It is also supposed to disrupt us and lead us to action.

DISRUPTING POWER TAKES PRACTICE

In Jesus' pre-entrance into ministry, he spent forty days in the wilderness, tempted to give into an unhealthy, enticing power. In the way the story's told, Satan tries to tempt Jesus to show his power in ways the world values—control, dominion, seized authority. Jesus resists, but we're often not able to. Henri Nouwen writes about this in his book on leadership, *In the Name of Jesus*, and says "What makes the temptation of power so seemingly irresistible? Maybe it is that power offers an easy substitute for the hard task of love. It seems easier to be God than to love God, easier to control people than to love people, easier to own life than to love life."[6]

Maybe power offers an easy substitute for the hard task of love. Jesus' example of humility and love over worldly power remains our deepest challenge.

The last week of his life, beginning with the triumphal entry into Jerusalem on a donkey, reveals it best. Over the years, I started to call Holy Week *It's Not What You Think Week* instead. Jesus—the promised king—who had been disrupting the status quo from top to bottom for several years, now enters Jerusalem to a roar of "hosannas!" and the thrill of impending victory. People were excited, inspired, drawn, hopeful. They were ready for him to kick butt, topple the empire, and restore justice the way they would. While Jesus started with turning over tables in the temple, as the week progresses, things radically shifted, and soon he was washing feet, talking about dying, and calling them to be one.

It wasn't long that the "hosannas" quickly shifted to "crucify him!"

Many of the same human dynamics are at play today, maybe now more than ever in the story of modern Christianity, our culture, and the world. In all shapes, sizes, and cultures, we are drawn to unhealthy power and charisma, to scapegoating, to divisive and exclusionary practices, and to perpetuating a myriad of conscious and unconscious strategies to resist and reject the Beatitudes-infused kind of power that Jesus embodied and preached.

History continues to prove that disrupting power is countercultural. There are a lot of obstacles, a lot of resistance to it, a lot to lose along the way. Yet, I believe we need to gather strength to forge a better path together, to *reimagine power,* to consider how, in the words misattributed to Mahatma Gandhi but inspiring nonetheless—"we can be the change we want to see in the world." Part of embodying change is respecting power as a crucial element of our life together; acknowledging that it's always present in every system, group, and relationship; and learning to use our personal and collective power humbly, wisely, and courageously.

I'm looking forward to wrestling along with you over the upcoming weeks. Anything I write is as much for me as it is for anyone reading it; it's never just about words on a page or head knowledge. It's about contemplative action and cultivating community. It's about practices, embodiment, and being willing to make mistakes, fail, and learn. It's about first healing ourselves and bringing that healing to the families, groups, teams, and systems we live and move in.

Even though I've spent the past eighteen years deep diving into conversations and practices to address issues of power as part of my faith community, The Refuge, which is a hub for healing community, social action, and creative collaboration, I always have so much more to learn. Yes, I'm a straight, married, white woman with a master's degree and children, and that is never lost on me in this conversation. However, I've also had my share of bumping up against unhealthy power as a female pastor in a male-dominated system and working for multiple decades in the margins alongside people who are disempowered by society in almost every way—being unhoused, addicted, struggling with mental illness, single parents, abuse survivors, generational poverty and race and class discrimination, LGBTQ+, and people with disabilities. Another twist is that my husband is from El Salvador, my kids are Brown, and I was raised by a single mom, always barely squeaking by financially. While I've learned a lot about shifting power over time, I continue to crawl, stumble, and bumble my way forward as well. Unhealthy power won't go down easily. In fact, it will fight with everything it's got to protect itself, and that's why sometimes change feels so frustratingly futile.

However, one of the reasons I still follow the ways of Jesus is that he shows us what is possible. He turns power on its head and challenges us to a life dedicated to the same. No matter what faith stream you come from or what you currently do or don't believe, most of us can agree on Jesus' subversiveness, his dedication to exposing and challenging destructive power, in systems and in us personally, and that he modeled what true power is—radical humility, even to death.

The kind of humility Jesus embodied wasn't the false kind that a lot of us learned in church: thinking of ourselves as lowly worms, miserable wretches, or disobedient sinners. The world doesn't need more people who don't recognize our personal power, our belovedness, our worth and value. It needs more people willing to step into who we were called to be—*forces for healing and hope in this fractured world.*

PREPARE TO BE CHALLENGED

This kind of subversive, countercultural, counterintuitive path is not for the fainthearted. It's not for those who get triggered easily by words like *privilege, patriarchy,* and *oppression.* It's not for people who quickly default to the words "but what about . . ." and constantly find a way to deflect responsibility from ourselves or prop up false equivalencies.

Turning Over Tables is for individuals and groups across genders, ages, life experiences, faith stories, and social demographics who want to engage in six-plus weeks of accessible, easy-to-digest daily reflections that center on power in a variety of ways. Each section will have a guiding theme—open, reveal, lament, repent, disrupt, cultivate, illuminate, embody, and sustain—to help us move through these weeks together. Our journey will include revealing how deeply issues of imbalanced power are embedded into us as humans and the systems we create, lamenting and grieving our contributions to harmful power or how we've diminished our own personal power, confession and healthy repentance, seeking new possibilities to embody healthy power, cultivating collaborative power through relationship and indigenous wisdom, illuminating the last week of Jesus' life, death, and resurrection, and exploring what these mean for our lives and today's social realities. While we can't unpack every aspect of power in the way it deserves in this short season together, we can open ourselves up to greater awareness that power dynamics are an undercurrent in most every aspect of our lives together and gain some language and practical ways to integrate change into our lives.

At the end of each week there are group reflection questions, prompts to help us grieve and lament (we can't skip over this part), actions and embodied practices to try individually and collectively, and prayers for action together. In the back of the book, there's a short section for church or organizational leaders hoping to shift power in their communities, as well as resources to explore far more deeply than we can in this space.

No matter where you are at in your faith story and whether you are on the underside of power, from a group traditionally marginalized because of race, gender, ability, economics, sexual orientation, relationship status, physical or mental disabilities, neurodivergence, body size, or other realities, I hope these words will strengthen and empower you. Please take care of yourself in any ways you need, recognizing that you know firsthand how power can be destructive.

If you're in a group that is typically on the upside of power, I am extra glad this book is in your hands! It is brave—and countercultural—to engage in this conversation and realities about power (and why this material might not be popular). However, I also want to warn you: it means that as you're reading you might feel anger or defensiveness or have the urge to close it and put it back on the shelf. I respect those feelings and have wrestled with knowing this might not feel like a traditional Lent devotional for some because it has less engagement with Bible verses and more reflections on how we live as part of wider culture beyond solely faith spaces. Discomfort is part of the Lenten season—and most certainly part of any power work—so let's welcome it, knowing that's what makes deeper transformation more possible.

My hope is that no matter where we're entering into this exploration of power we come humbly, find our own edges, listen to what is stirring up in us, and consider shifts in our lives and leadership that help heal and repair power differentials. It's an honor to walk alongside you this season, and I hope you can hang in there with me; I'm struck more than ever that disrupting entrenched power systems is lifelong personal, systemic, and spiritual work, and it's also extremely vulnerable.

Let's start with a deep breath, an open heart, and a posture of learning as we bravely honor our mortality, our relationship to power, and these human realities that are all tangled up together.

The First Days of Lent

OPEN

"There is within you a lamb and a lion. Spiritual maturity is the ability to let lamb and lion lie down together."
—Henri J. M. Nouwen[1]

Throughout Lent 2024, bombs were falling in Gaza, Palestine, and the death toll was surging past thirty thousand, with the majority being women and children. I have no idea where things will be by the time you're engaging with this material, but I do know that something shifted with the Israel-Hamas War that began October 7, 2023, in terms of greater international engagement on the realities of the Palestinian story and the pain of the Jewish community. So many of us, especially younger people, are experiencing a significant revealing of the oppression, complexity, and political entanglements involved in a new way. Eyes have been opened, hearts have been broken, and generational trauma has been revealed that has catalyzed a wide range of responses. Things feel dark, bleak, somewhat hopeless, and powerless.

Ash Wednesday, the entrance into the season of Lent and a day that millions of Christians of all shapes and sizes honor in a variety of ways, feels like the right space holder for some of these real and present feelings. I didn't grow up in a religious home, and some of these rhythms weren't part of my life until far into my spiritual journey. My grandparents were Catholic, and when I was young, I would stay with them for a few weeks every summer and attend mass. Honestly, I didn't really understand the whole experience and always felt behind the curve—the sitting, standing, reading, smells, bells, and the rote responses were foreign. Yet, I also remember experiencing something very grounding about it—the sense of everyone being on the same page, reverent, connected, inspired. When I started my own personal faith journey in college and my early years of marriage as a Christian, I landed in the nondenominational, attractional church world where there wasn't a liturgy or any connectedness to the church calendar. No one ever mentioned Ash Wednesday or the season of Lent, and Easter Sunday always just popped out of nowhere as the biggest, most exciting event of the year.

In that church culture, conversations about death, pain, and grief were either entirely skipped over or met with a response that if we prayed enough, believed enough, and trusted God enough, we could escape those hard feelings.

I didn't honor Ash Wednesday until The Refuge chose to do a liturgical year together in our first few years of existence, and I feel grateful for the simple and holy space of honoring the reality of my mortality, our mortality, and the humbling that creates. Receiving a cross of ashes on my forehead, reading Genesis 3:19, "you are dust, and to dust you shall return," felt hard at first but comforting too. In so many ways, the world's culture always wants to skip this hard, dusty, gloomy part of the human experience and get right to the "good stuff," which in Christian culture is often Easter and the resurrection. It's far more popular to focus on life and not death.

This is part of the social problem—both in and outside of faith spaces—and intersects with our addiction to unhealthy power. Most of us don't like to be humbled. We don't like to feel uncomfortable. We don't like to talk about death. And we certainly don't like to be called dust.

Yet, that's our starting place.

Not as people who are nothing, but as people who recognize our right size in the big story of the world: that we are humans, mere mortals, fragile, vulnerable, with a limited lifespan on this earth. This is what we have in common with every other human being on the planet, no matter which continent we live on or which religion we ascribe to. We're all going to physically die. *From dust we all came and to dust we shall return.*

Letting that sink in is lifetime work because a lot of us—especially those who may be steeped in a Christian theology that teaches us that because of God we are somehow better than others—have been conditioned to think that our faith somehow makes us more immune to calamity, insulate us from problems and pain, and make life easier (even though Jesus makes the opposite fairly clear). This has led a lot of people to separate from those who make us feel uncomfortable and to do all we can to stay on the mountaintop of life instead of walking in the lowlands of the valley.

When I visited Israel and Palestine years ago, we went to Judea, in the Jericho region of Israel, the place where Jesus spent forty days in the wilderness before beginning his public ministry. It is stark, rugged, and dusty land, and it makes sense it would be a place of wrestling, struggle, and revelation, where he would be confronted with temptation to give into unhealthy power as an escape.

Wrestling, struggle, revelation.

That's not only the story of Lent but also the story of progress, change, and social transformation. We need wrestling, struggle, and revelation to get to a new place in our own story, in the world's story.

As we launch into this first week together, I hope we can be open to what emerges. For these first few days, we're going to explore how easy it is to make ourselves too big or too small, to consider how power exists on a spectrum, and to see how a scarcity mentality related to power is central to its misuse. Hopefully, we're going to be open to change and possibility with a posture of openness to the Spirit moving through us, stirring, challenging, healing.

Father Thomas Keating says that "the process of conversion begins with genuine openness to change—openness to the possibility that just as natural life evolves, so too the spiritual life evolves."[2] We're evolving, the world's evolving, our faith is evolving. And this is why we need new eyes to see, new light to seek, new practices to embody. As we express our desire to see power more clearly and be open to possibility, may new light come, together.

What are you hoping to wrestle with this season?

ASH WEDNESDAY

Rightsized

"Let us strip off anything that slows us down or holds us back, and especially those sins that wrap themselves so tightly around our feet and trip us up."
                                                             —Hebrews 12:1 TLB

I've been going to 12-step meetings for over twenty years, and there's a recovery principle that has been extremely forming for me. In its simplest form, it's about *rightsizing ourselves—not making ourselves too big or too small.* Owning this, honoring this, is one of the healthiest things we can do to embody a different way of moving in the world. These kinds of simple spiritual truths are one of the many reasons I still go to meetings for codependence and the impacts of being an adult child of an alcoholic. In my experience, people in recovery seem to better recognize our humanness than in many other circles I've been in; the raw honesty that is present at every meeting keeps me coming back because I know I'm in good company with other humans who aren't trying to wriggle out of our humanness but, rather, face it head on.

Part of rightsizing ourselves as a principle in recovery is recognizing our tendency to make ourselves bigger than we really are—where we think we're better than others, smarter, more disciplined, more spiritual, more responsible than others, more . . . *whatever.* This "bigger and better than" mentality keeps us safe and protected, apart from others, superior to others, over others—and tired. At the same time, we can also do what many of us have been taught in unhealthy Christian systems or abusive families—believe that we are lower than others, smaller than others, not good enough, unworthy, have little to contribute and that we are nothing apart from a particular kind of theology. It might seem strange, but often, these two mentalities coexist!

Rightsizing is a solid starting principle and core thread to weave through this first week together as we hold space for today, Ash Wednesday, and our entrance into the Lenten season (or, if you're not utilizing this material specifically for Lent, your entrance into an intentional journey to engage with power either individually or with a group). There's not a time or season that isn't good for *rightsizing* ourselves, where we're not too big, not too small. I sometimes like to pause and remind myself that I'm just human like the rest of the world, made of flesh and blood, sure to take my last breath like every other human who ever existed and will ever exist in the future. Plus, it's good to remember that we're part of a story that started before us and will end after us. When we rightsize ourselves, we're no more or no less than others. We're human.

Unfortunately, culture and religion aren't the best at right-sizing and often reinforce all kinds of conflicting messages—that we're better than or worse than other people, less valuable than other people, more immune to pain or more powerful than other people. And because the deep grooves of racism, sexism, ageism, and ableism are intertwined in culture and religion, the result is often division and dissonance not only in our own personal experiences but also in the systems we are part of.

Days like Ash Wednesday, where we are confronted with our humanity, our mortality, can help equalize and ground us in a deeper truth. It helps remind us that we came from dust and we'll return to it. It can help us be more honest, humble, vulnerable, and rightsized, and these are the essential ingredients that are needed in conversations about power.

Dusty ones, this Ash Wednesday, let's humbly rightsize ourselves—not too big, not too small.

What does rightsizing yourself mean to you today?

THURSDAY

On a Spectrum

"Power–It's everywhere. Some seek or measure themselves by it, and some avoid or downplay it. Seldom do we pay attention to how having more or less power impacts relationships. . . . We grow our abilities to use our power for good or ill through many relationships and over a lifetime."

—Cedar Barstow[3]

Years ago, my friend Sasha, who leads Refuge Rainbow, our community's queer support group for youth and allies, did an LGBTQ+ Listen and Learn for our community. She shared how gender and sexuality is "fluid, flexible, and exists on a spectrum."[4]

Fluid, flexible, and exists on a spectrum.

As soon as she said it, I knew there was something about those three characteristics that described other areas of the human experience too.

When we're processing power this season, it's good to remember that issues of power are fluid, flexible, and exist on a spectrum. For some of us, we're in positions of power, leadership, or authority that are very clear in our work, but we may feel a differing range of power in those roles. Many of us may be white and financially resourced yet also find ourselves in a particular place in terms of power and society but because we're LGBTQ+, divorced, or neurodivergent. Others may come from groups that have been typically unempowered by our structures because of race, gender, age, socioeconomics, but are educationally privileged.

Power is fluid, flexible, and exists on a spectrum.

Faith is also fluid, flexible, and exists on a spectrum.

Embracing, honoring, and owning this helps us in these conversations because it reminds us that these issues are complex—personally and communally—and they are always running as an undercurrent in all our experiences.

For some of us, we have power in one role or reality and far less in another. We might have positional power because of our vocation but little to no sense of personal power in other relationships. If we're aging, we might feel a lack of power at this stage of our story but remember the days when we held it.

As we rightsize ourselves in the human story, begin looking honestly at ourselves and the cultures we are in, and explore the unique realities we are all experiencing, I hope we'll let ourselves be open to engaging with power as a living, breathing, evolving reality that needs attention, reckoning, and healing.

Let's embrace the wide range of ways we engage with our own personal power, relational power, positional power, and spiritual power and honor that they are all at play in our stories. It's comforting—and challenging—to remember that as people of faith and hope, we can help justice and equity flow more freely and fully for everyone, not just ourselves.

As we wrestle with power together in the days and weeks to come, we can draw on the reality that power is fluid, flexible, and exists on a spectrum.

Reflect on where you've been in the past in relationship to power and where you might be now.

FRIDAY

Power Is Not like Pie

"Then Jesus took the loaves, and when he had given thanks he distributed them to those who were seated; so also the fish, as much as they wanted. When they were satisfied, he told his disciples, 'Gather up the fragments left over, so that nothing may be lost.' So they gathered them up, and from the fragments of the five barley loaves, left by those who had eaten, they filled twelve baskets."

— John 6:11–13

Oh humans, we love to make things comfortable, predictable, measurable, finite! When it comes to power, we often think of it as a limited resource (there's only so much) or as being a certain size (bigger is better). We think of it like a pie: the more guests you serve, the smaller each piece must be. We think that when someone gets more power, it means someone else has to get less. This scarcity mindset about power runs deep.

This is why when people in the dominant group consider any underrepresented group stepping into greater leadership, capacity, or resourcing in some way, they often default to thinking, *What does this mean for me? What will I lose?* At the same time, I have seen some people who were traditionally unempowered get a new role or position and immediately begin to overpower others, making rules they themselves would have hated and taking as much power as they could as quickly as possible. It's fascinating.

It's because we often think power is like pie.

Fortunately, power is far more like loaves and fishes.

There's this wild, beautiful, and miraculous thing that can happen when we share power together and make room for all of us—*it multiplies.*

When we believe power is like pie and there are only so many slices, someone's always going to go hungry, and that's most likely the person or group with the least power. When I was the only female leader on a big church staff where power was treated like pie, I would always feel the sense of knowing I was going to get only the crumbs left in the pan; and that frequently happened. I was the one who could do the announcements but not preach from the front, come to meetings but never lead them, work my tail off on a project but not get the credit.

The upside-down ways of Jesus were always about shaking up power: challenging dysfunctional religious leaders; denouncing fear and control, which is a driving force of unhealthy power; and admonishing people for adopting a spirit of scarcity instead of abundance. He consistently disrupted the systems of power that keep people divided, oppressed, and imprisoned.

After forty days in the wilderness, Jesus began his three years of stirring the pot on power, starting with these words from the Jewish prophet Isaiah:

> "The Spirit of the Lord is on me,
> because he has anointed me
> to proclaim good news to the poor.
> He has sent me to proclaim freedom for the prisoners
> and recovery of sight for the blind,
> to set the oppressed free,
> to proclaim the year of the Lord's favor."
> (Luke 4:18–19 NIV)

Four chapters later he fed five thousand people with five loaves and two fish.

Whether you believe all the alleged facts of the story or not, one thing that prevails about Jesus (not "the church") is that he was dedicated to dismantling fear, control, and self-protection so that people could be liberated, free, and equal.

Sure, most everything still operates on the scarcity concept of power being like pie.

But seeing power through a new lens that opens our eyes and heart, power becomes much more like loaves and fishes that empower the many while disempowering no one.

How have you intersected with power from a scarcity mindset?

SATURDAY

Pause and Ponder: What's Opening in You?

We covered a few core ideas in a short amount of time this entry week: rightsizing ourselves, holding that power is fluid, flexible, and exists on a spectrum; and remembering that power is not finite or scarce. These may not be the lessons you expected at the start of a Lenten journey, but they will help us as we step into next week. Remember, these first few days are focused on being open—open about our own story and experiences as we begin to connect with power, open to noticing where we might feel our bodies constrict or where we might feel relief, open to the Spirit's stirring, open to learn, and open to keep engaging and growing. We've touched on some big topics, and now it's time to pause, ponder, and reflect on what emerged for us in these first few days before we move into our first full week—where the realities of misused power are revealed more clearly, together.

Wrestle, Reflect, Engage

Reflection Questions

1. Looking back on this first week together, what words, phrases, or concepts emerged for you? What resonated?
2. Share how the idea of rightsizing might help you with entering into the season of Lent this year. How can you let go of thinking of yourself as "too big" or "too small"?
3. Reflect on the idea of power being more like loaves and fishes than pie. How would some of the groups and systems you are part of look differently if that reality was more present?
4. What is your intention this season related to power, and in what ways are you hoping to grow?

Prompts for Grief and Gratitude

Don't overthink these questions. Use them as a guide to engage with simple unedited honesty just for yourself.

- When it comes to rightsizing, I know I've made myself too _____ and/or too _____, and I am sad that it's created these impacts in my life and work: _____.
- As I consider my relationship with power and the first week of reflections, I'm grateful that I've _____.

Actions and Practices

1. Go outside at night and spend some time looking up at the stars, the moon, the dark sky, considering the vastness of the universe and our humble position in it. Notice how that feels.
2. With a pen and piece of paper (or markers, crayons, colored pencils if you'd like), sketch images that reflect power that's finite and scarce (like pie) and exponential and multiplying (like loaves and fishes). If images feel hard to draw, write words that describe each. Consider groups, systems, relationships that you have been or are part of. When it comes to power, what have they been more like? Write or draw words that describe what it was like to be part of them.
3. Begin to open your eyes this week to power at play in the circles you live and move in. Tune in and notice what you observe, feel, are concerned about, and are challenged by.

God, Spirit, Advocate,
keep revealing truths where we are blind;
keep healing us where we are wounded;
keep moving us forward when we are afraid.
May we remain humble, open, vulnerable
as we keep seeing power more clearly together.
Amen.

Week One

REVEAL

Then they began to argue among themselves about who would be the greatest among them. Jesus told them, "In this world the kings and great men lord it over their people, yet they are called 'friends of the people.' But among you it will be different. Those who are the greatest among you should take the lowest rank, and the leader should be like a servant. Who is more important, the one who sits at the table or the one who serves? The one who sits at the table, of course. But not here! For I am among you as one who serves."

—Luke 22:24–27 NLT

One of the biggest lies I was taught in my early years of faith was that Christians had something that everyone else was missing. Anyone who didn't believe, behave, or belong in a certain way were somehow less-than and needed help, needing saving; we were at the top of the social heap.

Tangled into this lie was that people who were American, white, able-bodied, economically resourced, neurotypical, married, and straight were better too. In that culture, those things were the goal, the blessing, the set of characteristics that set us apart from everyone else. My first inclination as I write these words is to want to minimize it, wondering if maybe I'm overstating or exaggerating. But that's the problem with power—*we often don't want to address it honestly and directly.*

The other thing we often don't want to do is engage in our true history—not the whitewashed one most of us were taught, where the dominant power narrative is always at the center. For the most part, we weren't taught an unbiased history in schools to start with. Why? Because world history is most often told by the winners. I was confronted directly with this when I learned about the Doctrine of Discovery, going all the way back to 1452 and 1455, when Pope Nicholas V issued two papal bulls that essentially say that Christian explorers encountering indigenous people in the lands they "discover" should *conquer them all, destroy them all,* and *subdue them all.*[1] This deep entanglement of oppressive power and domination is embedded in our world and faith history. Add to that the idea of Manifest Destiny, a false construct of North American colonization that says there's a whole group of Christian people who are meant to prosper at all costs to others, and it really is a hot mess of destructive power in God's name. The message is clear: we are better, and *we deserve to keep whatever we find.*

These are lies.

Over many generations, these lies have subtly and overtly led some of us to believe we're better than others—especially if we're white, economically resourced, Christian, able-bodied, thin, and straight, which are the typical "top" of the social systems. Others of you might identify with living and moving on the underside of the dominant power systems as a person of color, neurodivergent, unmarried, LGBTQ+, with a physical disability, or more, and you may have received the message that you are somehow less-than.

These lies affect us all.

Healing requires acknowledging the lies we've been taught, discovering how deep they are in our collective unconscious, and seeing the ways they are showing up today so that we can untangle from them. We must break out of denial and see more clearly that, even though we've made strides in the areas of racial, gender, and LGBTQ+ equality, we are far from an equitable society for all people. Take one look at the 2016–24 US election cycles, and you can see how the lie of "who's better" isn't subtle but painfully magnified and used to divide and foster fear and dominance. It sadly reveals how deep the beliefs of who belongs, who deserves to be here, and whose safety matters permeates so many people's thinking.

I remember in my early days as a Christian how I, too, was sucked into the culture that taught me false messages about people on welfare taking advantage of the system, about LGBTQ+ people being out of God's will, and that women were meant to be underneath the power and authority of their husbands (and that having a husband and children were signs of superiority too!). Ugh, it's ugly to think about some of the things I believed! All of this was *in the name of God*, which, frankly, makes it even more painful as I look back on that season of my story. I know I'm not alone in getting sucked into cultures that are built on exclusion. The irony is that exclusion was the exact thing Jesus railed against yet is promoted by so many groups in his name.

It's important for us to understand that these false and destructive narratives that create oppressive power aren't a thing of the past—they're showing up subtly and overtly in how we feel about ourselves and how we feel about others. *Being better* is rooted in our attachment to a false sense of control, and control is a primary ingredient in power. Richard Rohr says it well: "Christians are usually sincere and well-intentioned people until you get to any real issues of ego, control, power, money, pleasure, and security. Then they tend to be pretty much like everybody else." He adds that it's because of our focus on "a bogus version of the Gospel, some fast-food religion, without any deep transformation of the self; and the result has been the spiritual disaster of 'Christian' countries that tend to be as consumer-oriented, proud, warlike, racist, class conscious, and addictive as everybody else—and often more so, I am afraid."[2]

As we travel through this first full week together, we are going to confront these realities with an openness from last week and a desire to see more clearly and notice more intentionally how deep the undercurrent of power exists so that greater truth can be revealed. It makes me think of the story in Mark 10 of Bartimaeus, a blind man from Jericho who was sitting by the roadside when Jesus and his disciples came by. He began to shout, "Jesus, Son of David, have mercy on me!" Significantly, the people around him "rebuked" him, telling him to shut up, but the passage said that "he shouted all the more, 'Son of David, have mercy on me!'" (vv. 47–48 NIV).

I love what Jesus did next: he asked what Bartimaeus wanted him to do, and Bartimaeus replied, "Rabbi, I want to see."

I want to see.

In this story, Jesus restored Bartimaeus's sight and told him "Your faith has healed you" (vv. 51–52 NIV).

I do not think our sight will be immediately restored when it comes to the realities of power; we'll be wrestling with this forever. But I do think that truths are revealed to us along the way that help shift our hearts, minds, and practices—truths that transform our faith and change the way we move and live in the world. We can discover our own blind spots and treat these discoveries as a gift instead of a personal critique, as a catalyzer for growth instead of something to be afraid of.

The wise words of Richard Rohr are crucial here, "You cannot heal what you do not first acknowledge."[3]

We can't have transformation without truth.

In considering power, what do you want to see more clearly?

MONDAY

The Danger in Denial

"Not everything that is faced can be changed, but nothing
can be changed until it is faced."
—James Baldwin[4]

Years ago, when I was on the megachurch staff that was
wrought with unhealthy power dynamics, I tried to encourage
leaders to face those dynamics directly. I had concerns about
unchecked power that the all-male elder board held over our
four-thousand-member church that was reeling from a moral
scandal involving the founding pastor. In my role as the adult
ministry pastor, I asked if I could attend their early morning
meeting to offer feedback and gain some clarity. As I sat alone
facing them in their line of chairs together, I shared my unease
that they weren't acknowledging how much power they held
over the church in this season; they were making immense
directional decisions without input from our ministry team or
the wider community.

I directly said to the lead elder, who held the most power
and sway, "I don't know if you realize how much power you
have." He looked at me straight in the eye, raised his voice,
and bellowed, "What do you mean? I don't have any more
power than you do!" It makes me laugh on one level, how
ridiculous that statement is, denying the power differential
between a white, male, sixty-year-old evangelical executive
and a thirty-six-year-old female leader who had to fight for the
title of pastor; however, his words are far from funny. This
kind of typical denial about power is what prevents change
we desperately need. It also resonates with what the prophet
Jeremiah admonishes, "You can't heal a wound by saying it's
not there!" (6:14 TLB).

When we pretend that power dynamics don't exist, it's
dangerous. When we hold on to a false belief that our society
treats us as all equal (even though that's what we wish for),

it's dangerous. When we refuse to acknowledge imbalanced power in our systems and structures, it's dangerous. When we deny our own personal power and how it impacts others in the groups we are part of, it's dangerous.

I fully understand why denial is our first response. It's a simple form of self-protection that shields us from the need to engage with the painful realities of disparate power, whether it's in our own relationships and roles or in the wider systems we're part of. While there's straight-up denial like the head elder expressed in our conversation, there are more subtle forms of denial too. These can include minimizing, generalizing, and rationalizing. Do any of these patterns sound familiar to you when it comes to trying to avoid engaging with painful things?

They sure do for me: I often want to minimize the impact of my power as a white, straight, educated woman by speaking in detached generalities and rationalizing my good intentions. At the same time (because there are usually always several angles at play when it comes to power), I have often denied how I have minimized my personal power to adjust to fit in patriarchal systems and pretend it's not as painful as it really is. *You can't heal a wound you say isn't there.* Denial is dangerous. As Heather McGhee, the author of *The Sum of Us*, says, "Denial leaves people ill-prepared to function or thrive in a diverse society."[5] When we avoid confronting our own truth, we don't develop the skills to own our dissonant feelings in a healthy way or build capacity to hold differences in tension. Our path forward requires that we soften our self-protected hearts, recognize the scales on our eyes, and begin looking at power more honestly, soberly, bravely. It's what Jesus spent a lot of time calling us to. It's what all important anti-oppression work starts with. It's how healing begins.

What are some wounds about power
and your story that are hard to acknowledge?

TUESDAY

Intersections

"Intersectionality operates as both the observance and analysis of power imbalances, and the tool by which those power imbalances could be eliminated altogether."
—Jane Coaston[6]

Coined by professor Kimberlé Crenshaw in 1989, the principle of *intersectionality* is not a new concept but has become more of a buzzword over the years (which was never her intention) and certainly always needs consideration in any reflections about power. The hierarchies that society establishes for race, gender, socioeconomics, age, sexual orientation, and physical abilities always intersect. Intersectionality means that a gay Black man has a different experience and different level of power than a straight Black man or that a female with a disability may face more gender discrimination than an able-bodied woman. These layers impact each other and are tangled up with each other, and healing and change is not possible without acknowledging that. Crenshaw says it this way: "Intersectionality is a lens through which you can see where power comes and collides, where it interlocks and intersects. It's not simply that there's a race problem here, a gender problem here, and a class or LBGTQ problem there. Many times that framework erases what happens to people who are subject to all of these things."[7]

While power is complex, we have a natural tendency to want to simplify it. Culture likes to lump people into one category and make assumptions about everyone in the category as the same, while intersectionality honors the deeper reality that needs attention.

I love conversations about intersectionality because they give room for nuance, reality, and greater illumination of what is at play. Unfortunately, instead of letting ideas of intersectionality and greater awareness of power differentials and social inequities expand and inform us, some people have misinterpreted intersectionality as a threat to their power. (Remember, the belief that power is like pie runs deep).

Appreciating intersectionality doesn't mean I always embed it in my practices, though. I often go to the path of least resistance first, which tends to be labeling someone by what is most definable on the surface. In my work at The Refuge, I engage with people experiencing homelessness on a regular basis, and it's easy to sometimes lump everyone into one category—homeless. Yet, I've got to continually remind myself that the experiences for my friend Evan, who is white, transgender, neurodivergent, and in their thirties are completely different than for Tan, who is a senior citizen immigrant of color. It's hard because it takes more time, more pause, more reflection. Yet our work together is to not give in to visible labels and assumptions but instead, in relationship, uncover the multiple layers of humanity and social realities that lie underneath our first assumptions.

My daughter, who is Latina, a dentist, thirty years old, and an officer in the military, crosses a wide range of power dynamics in her work in the world. We always talk about the compounding factors of our unique stories and how they intersect with power and leadership.

This is why humanizing all our experiences is so crucial.

And that's why recognizing intersectionality is so revealing.

What are some layers of your life, experiences, and realities that often get ignored because people don't see beyond the surface?

WEDNESDAY

The P-Word—Privilege

"I have come to see white privilege as an invisible package
of unearned assets that I can count on cashing in each day,
but about which I was 'meant' to remain oblivious."
—Peggy McIntosh[8]

Years ago, after Michael Brown was killed by police in Ferguson,
Missouri, I attended several multifaith gatherings in Denver
centered on collective antiracism work. I will never forget a
conversation at one of the tables with other clergy across faiths
where leaders shared that if they said the words *white privilege*
in their predominantly white and financially resourced congre-
gations, they would most certainly immediately lose members
and their community's livelihood could be at risk. Privilege,
which I sometimes call the P-word because it has such a negative connotation in many circles, is not something we should
be afraid of. It's not a threat. It's not a judgment. It's just
a reality: white privilege, male privilege, straight privilege,
economic privilege, able-bodied privilege are real.

Peggy McIntosh, a professor whose work on white privilege
has been widely shared, says that "White privilege is like an
invisible weightless knapsack of special provisions, maps, pass-
ports, codebooks, visas, clothes, tools and blank checks."[9]

When I first encountered the topic of privilege, I remember
feeling the initial dissonance too: *Wait, what? My mom was
a single mom, my dad didn't make it past ninth grade in high
school and was a lifelong alcoholic, I struggled and strived to
pay my way through college and change the course of history for
my family. How could where I got in my life be privileged?* As I
engaged in more honest reflection and challenge in antiracism
work, I was confronted with the reality of my whiteness, my
able-bodiedness, my education—all things that were in my
"invisible knapsack" of privilege and give me power in certain
situations that others do not have.

Privilege is not something to be ashamed of. We do not need to feel guilty for being white, male, or straight or having money in the bank; that's not the idea here. But it is the easiest place for us to default and escape from doing the deeper work. We each are who we are, were born how we were born. But I want to be someone who understands the power that comes from privilege instead of pretending it doesn't exist or shoo it away as someone else's problem. The work that needs to be done in our hearts is to honor how privilege automatically gives us a certain kind of power.

Yes, in the kingdom of God, there should be no white privilege, male privilege, straight privilege, economic privilege. But the kingdom of God never drops out of the sky; it takes a lot of work to create it here on earth, and it's up against the exact same things Jesus was up against two thousand years ago—privilege and power and the ways they divide.

When you hear the word privilege, *what does it stir up in you?*

THURSDAY

Tangled in Supremacist Logic

"Everybody wants to rule the world."
—Tears for Fears[10]

The first time I heard my friend Melvin Bray share a list of "supremacies" that were at the heart of inequity, something deep in my soul was touched, and I knew that this list would transform some of the ways I viewed power. I also knew I was busted. He had named supremacies, which I didn't have language for, at play underneath the surface of my beliefs in relationship to others. As an author, advocate, and organizational consultant, his work is centered on "unlearning inequity," and he shared at an online workshop that The Refuge hosted on how "supremacist logic" is embedded in us through the culture, families, faith systems, and social structures we've been part of.[11]

Supremacies are a false form of power and are centered on what he calls our "addiction to being on top." In the workshop, he listed these: *white supremacy, male supremacy, straight supremacy, Christian supremacy, able-bodied supremacy, and economic supremacy.*[12] Most of us have some combination of supremacies embedded in us, a belief of being better than others that is often unconscious but always present in how we think and act. I appreciated how he shared, as a Black man raised to be a pastoral leader, that he's always untangling himself from the lie of male supremacy and Christian supremacy too. Again, these are not exclusive to only one demographic; there are always so many intersections.

Melvin's work includes modifying the 12 steps of recovery into what he calls the Truth and Transformation Model, using their wisdom and framework to help all individuals and systems create greater equity. Personal transformation affects systemic transformation, and systemic transformation affects personal transformation. They are intertwined together.

The first step in the Truth and Transformation Model is this:

> We admit that supremacist logic in sundry forms has been core to Western culture as a whole as well as in the development of our own particular nation, society, community, and sense of self, and whereas we are powerless to control the people and circumstances into which we are born and the ways they have shaped us, we do have the power to change its persistently inequitable outcomes.[13]

There's a lot in there to consider and wrestle with, and this is what we use as a guide in our Practicing Equity in Recovery group at The Refuge. Acknowledging how deep these supremacies run is humbling, painful, and enlightening. For me, I am grieved that I was over fifty years old before this concept began seeping into my mind, heart, and soul. But I'm grateful it finally did; untangling from it is lifetime work. *While "we are powerless to control the people and circumstances into which we are born and the ways they have shaped us, we do have the power to change its persistently inequitable outcomes."*

This was Jesus' call, and it's our work to do.

What are some of the supremacies you identify with?

FRIDAY

The Other P-Word–Patriarchy

"Patriarchy is not counter-cultural. It has for centuries been the norm. What's truly counter-cultural is imitating Jesus, who, 'being in very nature God,' surrendered his power and privilege to become a human—one birthed, nursed, protected, befriended, and BELIEVED by women."
—Rachel Held Evans[14]

Just like the P-word *privilege* we touched on a few days ago, there's another P-word we can't step over on this path of engaging with power: *patriarchy*! Since the beginning of time, patriarchal structures are bedrock in most all world cultures and world religions. One doesn't have to be a history major to notice male domination and female subjugation in all generations of human cultures. I know it's not exclusive, and you may be saying, "but what about the queens?" Yes, female leaders have sporadically ruled, but an individual's reign is different than transforming the dominant culture.

Almost all issues related to inequitable power are paved with patriarchy, and it is embedded into all parts of our society, whether it's acknowledged or not. Untangling from it is more than equal pay, women in higher levels of leadership, and better access to opportunities. It's about recognizing that everything is built on a visible and often invisible male privilege that affects us even if we don't think it does.

Patriarchy hurts men and women alike. It limits us. It saps our human dignity.

And, like almost anything we process related to power, we want to squirm our way out of confronting it. As a female writing these words, hoping they will challenge and heal, I also feel patriarchy in my bones in almost every word I write—
Will this be acceptable to men? Am I saying it too strongly? Am I pushing too hard? How can I adjust to make it not feel so harsh?

Ugh, bleh, ick! But these are candid manifestations of how patriarchy sneaks into almost everything and is always running in the background.

If we are going to engage with breaking out of denial and opening our souls to new revelations that form and change us, then all of us—male, female, nonbinary alike—need to reckon with the damage that patriarchy has done to all of us and that is at the root of all the "supremacies." And the church, instead of leading the way on this, has actually been one of the absolute worst examples, upholding patriarchy and limiting the freedom of women, Black, indigenous, and people of color (BIPOC), and LGBTQ+ folks since its beginning.

I used to spend a lot of time talking about smashing the patriarchy (and I still believe it needs to be smashed), but I came to realize that it's often so deep, tall, wide, thick, and seemingly impenetrable, that smashing isn't going to cut it. But what we can do, what's available to us now, is what Jesus always inspired: playing our part in subverting the dominant system to create something better.

No matter your gender, faith, or circumstance,
how have you been harmed by patriarchy?

SATURDAY

Pause and Ponder: What's Being Revealed?

It's not lost on me that we are covering a lot of ground in a short amount of time on this limited journey together. Entire books can be written on each of these compact reflections, but my hope is that we let go of thinking we have to deep dive into every day and somehow figure this power thing out. It's far more complex than that, and this material is meant for us to expand our experience in ways we can this season and hopefully let our souls not just be stirred but moved to action as well. We can't have transformation without truth, and I hope we can continue to maintain a posture of a bended knee, an open heart, a willing soul that knows that the lies of supremacist logic are damaging our society and contrary to the ways of Jesus.

My guess is we are all wrestling with different things when we consider our relationship to power, especially through our unique lenses of being on the upside or underside of it. Maybe we're disillusioned about the false history we've been taught and how easy it was to buy it because of our privilege. Or maybe we're noticing how we've harmed others as leaders in a patriarchal system or how we've been harmed and disempowered by it. Maybe we have anger toward the faith systems we have been attached to that perpetuated a damaging narrative of superiority at the expense of others. Whatever has been revealed (and to whatever degree you're feeling it), it's important to honor, acknowledge, and let it sink in.

Lament is part of our path forward, and it leads us to repentance, turning away from what's keeping destructive patterns of power in place. Lament is an action. It's a catalyzer, a propelling emotion that helps us get unstuck, and that's what we'll engage with next.

Wrestle, Reflect, Engage

Reflection Questions

1. As you look back on this week, what are some of the takeaways that emerged for you or specific words, phrases, feelings?
2. Reflect on what is being revealed to you in this season of your story related to power and privilege? What are you learning?
3. In your Christian or family culture, were you taught that you were better than others? In what ways? How did that false belief separate you from others?
4. Read the first step from Melvin Bray's Truth and Transformation Model (p. 37): "We admit that supremacist logic in sundry forms has been core to Western culture as a whole as well as in the development of our own particular nation, society, community, and sense of self, and whereas we are powerless to control the people and circumstances into which we are born and the ways they have shaped us, we do have the power to change its persistently inequitable outcomes." What words or phrases connect with you? Why?

Prompts for Grief and Gratitude

- It pains me that I was taught that I was/we were better than _____.

- I am sad that the lies of white supremacy, male supremacy, Christian supremacy, etc. are embedded into my faith and experience and have caused _____.

- I'm thankful for _____ for helping my eyes to be opened to a more honest reflection about our history and a possible path forward.

Actions and Practices

1. Learn more about the Doctrine of Discovery and how tangled up Christianity is in world domination.
2. Talk to a friend, family member, or safe clergyperson about what you are learning right now in your anti-oppression work, what you're wrestling with, and how you're transforming your beliefs about equity.
3. Watch Kimberlé Crenshaw's TED Talk–"The Urgency of Intersectionality."
4. Find a copy of a wheel of power/privilege online and study it, noticing the different elements of power it might include—skin color, education, ability, sexuality, neurodiversity, mental health, body size, housing, wealth, language, gender, citizenship. Where do you fit in?

God,
give us courage to wrestle, reflect, and engage
with power in new ways.
Keep helping us break out of denial.
May we denounce false teachings that harm.
May we open ourselves to truth that transforms.
May we maintain a posture of humility and hope
as we keep transforming together.
Amen.

Week Two

LAMENT

"In lament, our task is never to convince someone of the brokenness of this world; it is to convince them of the world's worth in the first place. True lament is not born from that trite sentiment that the world is bad but rather from a deep conviction that it is worthy of goodness."
—Cole Arthur Riley[1]

Years ago, we hosted a Native American Learning Workshop at The Refuge with Mark Charles, a Navajo writer, pastor, and activist. His book with coauthor Soong-Chan Rah, *Unsettling Truths: The Ongoing, Dehumanizing Legacy of the Doctrine of Discovery*, is an excellent resource for people seeking to look more honestly at our nation's history and the church's complicity in the decimation of indigenous people as part of our quest for freedom. It's not for the fainthearted, and I will always remember a conversation Mark and I had after the gathering, where he shared pointedly about the reality *that everyone wants to do something when it comes to social justice, but no one wants to lament.* We can't move to better action until we first allow ourselves to grieve and lament the ravages of destructive power in our society and in our faith systems, politics, and culture. There's a difference between personal lament and communal lament, but they are intertwined, and we'll be engaging with both this week.

I am no stranger to personal lament. After losing our nineteen-year-old son to suicide in 2019, lament has become my friend. Allowing ourselves to feel the magnitude of grief and loss has been the hardest work of my family's lives, and through practice, we keep learning how to metabolize grief as a natural part of the human experience. When it comes to lament related to destructive power in systems, it can feel more nebulous. However, the deeper I engage in spaces and places that allow for open and honest conversations about the lies of white, Christian, male, able-bodied, straight, economically resourced supremacies, the more I see the magnitude of damage from these unhealthy systems. It often makes me feel sick to my stomach, and that's not because I'm soft or weak or too sensitive; it is because it is, indeed, sickening how misused power harms, kills, destroys, and tries to diminish human dignity.

The same destructive power that Jesus was railing against two thousand years ago is still at play today: religious systems that exclude and oppress, political systems that harm and neglect, race and gender norms that limit and discriminate, and social systems that are bent against the people that need them the most. It can sometimes feel as if we're powerless to do something about it, but we're not. However, no movement is possible without breaking out of denial and self-protection and allowing the magnitude of dysfunctional patterns related to power to be revealed. Bizzy Feekes says, "We don't lament just to be sad, but instead to help us understand that things are not the way they should be by uncovering truths about life as we know it."[2]

This week as we engage with lament, my hope is always that we'll engage however we each need based on our unique contexts and stories. It may be centered on ways we have misused power over others or how we have not stepped into our own healthy power out of fear and insecurity. It might be sorrow over how we have not used our voice on behalf of others because we're scared of the repercussions, or grief about the perpetual abuse of power that's happened throughout history into today that makes us feel disgusted and powerless. It can be related to the revelation of how much we've invested ourselves in being better or worse than others. Regardless of which form grief and lament takes, it is important to allow ourselves to engage with the pain and avoid trying to disconnect from the soul and guts part because we *don't want to go there.*

It's human to avoid pain, but acknowledging and honoring reality, feeling feelings that need to be felt, and allowing grief to move through us open us up to health and action. It's also a big part of trauma-informed practices, which are central to any work that involves shifting power. Stuffing feelings, disconnecting from pain out of self-protection, denial, and avoidance all create more problems. Finding ways to honor truth and express ourselves freely helps metabolize trauma and reduce its negative impact individually and communally.

The work of Resmaa Menakem, a trauma therapist who has written several excellent books on racial trauma, is incredibly helpful, and he shares the difference between "dirty pain" (avoidance) and "clean pain" (healthy acknowledgment), and he shows that "a key factor in the perpetuation of white-body supremacy is many people's refusal to experience clean pain around the myth of race. Instead, usually out of fear, they choose the dirty pain of silence and avoidance and, invariably, prolong the pain."[3] Although we're talking about not only white-body supremacy in our reflections on power, Menakem's observations about it apply to all the different supremacies (race, gender, economic, abilities) we're wrestling with too.

Dirty pain of silence and avoidance is also hypocritical. It's pretending that nothing's wrong when it is. It makes me think of the rebuking words that Jesus shares to the crowd and his disciples along with seven woes toward the teachers of the law in Matthew 23. He starts with "The teachers of the law and the Pharisees sit in Moses' seat. So you must be careful to do everything they tell you. But do not do what they do, for they do not practice what they preach. They tie up heavy, cumbersome loads and put them on other people's shoulders, but they themselves are not willing to lift a finger to move them" (vv. 2–4 NIV). Then he starts with the woes; here are just a few of them. Strap in—they're rough.

"Woe to you, teachers of the law and Pharisees, you hypocrites! You shut the door of the kingdom of heaven in people's faces. You yourselves do not enter, nor will you let those enter who are trying to." (v. 13 NIV)

"Woe to you, teachers of the law and Pharisees, you hypocrites! You give a tenth of your spices—mint, dill and cumin. But you have neglected the more important matters of the law—justice, mercy and faithfulness. You should have practiced the latter, without neglecting the former. You blind guides! You strain out a gnat but swallow a camel." (vv. 23–24 NIV)

"Woe to you, teachers of the law and Pharisees, you hypocrites! You clean the outside of the cup and dish, but inside they are full of greed and self-indulgence. Blind Pharisee! First clean the inside of the cup and dish, and then the outside also will be clean." (vv. 25–26 NIV)

"Woe to you, teachers of the law and Pharisees, you hypocrites! You are like whitewashed tombs, which look beautiful on the outside but on the inside are full of the bones of the dead and everything unclean. In the same way, on the outside you appear to people as righteous but on the inside you are full of hypocrisy and wickedness." (vv. 27–28 NIV)

It's easy to think that he's just talking about the Pharisees, not us, and maybe if we're not in leadership we're even more off the hook. But we don't get a free pass. We all have pieces of these human tendencies in us in different ways, and this journey is about engaging with them.

Personal and community lament is a path forward for us together, not to beat ourselves up, impose false shame on ourselves, or endure it so that we can say we paid our pain penance. Rather, it's about allowing ourselves to honor the magnitude of unhealthy power's damage to people's faith, humanity, culture, and identity. It's part of our path forward, together.

This week we're going to open to lament, to glean from the wisdom of 12-step recovery and how that kind of raw honesty can help us to engage with grief and shame, to honor how some of us have been abused by power ourselves, diminished our own personal power, and grieve ways we've impacted others even when it wasn't our intent. It's just another fun week together, ha! But this is our work and why we're here this season: to not look away from unhealthy power in ourselves and the systems we're part of, to not try to squirm out of responsibility, to not minimize or rationalize, but to allow ourselves to lament and practice "clean pain." That's our best hope and most certainly is what our divided and broken world needs more of.

How can you make greater room for lament
instead of trying to skip forward to action?

MONDAY

Inventory

"Blessed are those who mourn,
  for they will be comforted."
                                        —Matthew 5:4 NIV

In the traditional 12 steps, the fourth and fifth steps are often the scariest for people even though they are two of the most healing and transformational. The colloquial wording for them across versions goes like this: Step 4—*We made a searching and fearless moral inventory of ourselves* and Step 5—*We admitted to God, ourselves, and someone we trust the exact nature of our wrongs.*[4]

Although many associate the 12 steps with only drugs and alcohol, I firmly believe they are an incredible tool for transformation related to power, control, shame, insecurity, and a host of other patterns that cause us and others harm. Honest reflection is not to reduce us to a puddle of shame and regret; it's about examining ourselves, humbling ourselves, and bravely confronting patterns in our lives that do not lead to peace. It's why I put my butt in the chair at the 12-step meeting at The Refuge year after year. I'm in awe of the healing that happens in a simple circle with a group of people across almost every imaginable difference with a common purpose—to change unhealthy patterns.

A "searching and fearless moral inventory" related to power might look like admitting ways we have bought into lies of the different supremacies, ways we've diminished our own personal power out of fear, overpowered others to get what we want, used power and control to cover up insecurity and self-doubt, or disempowered people we love so that we could feel better about ourselves and allow ourselves to feel the pain of our actions.

The other part about this step is to remember healing work is never a "one and done." We don't do an inventory and never come back to it. In fact, Step 10 reminds us that *we continued to take personal inventory, and when we were wrong promptly admitted it.* It reminds me of several other Beatitudes: "Blessed are the pure in heart, for they will see God. Blessed are the peacemakers, for they will be called children of God " (Matthew 5:8–9). Note, it says *peacemakers*, not *peacekeepers*. Peacekeeping is what most of us have been taught and why we often don't address these issues directly.

This way of the 12 steps and Jesus' words are intertwined. They don't make sense in a culture that values power, control, hierarchy, and patriarchy, but in the wild ways of Jesus, they are the center.

Today, it can help to embrace the idea that our work isn't to clear out in one fell swoop all the ways we've misused power, minimized our own power, or been harmed by power. That's not how healing and recovery work. What we can do is allow ourselves some space for brave reflection that continues to deepen and expand as we confront our relationship with power more honestly and learn to mourn instead of avoid.

*What's a way you've diminished your own power
or overpowered others?*

TUESDAY

Abused by Power

#MeToo #ChurchToo

When Brett Kavanaugh was being confirmed for his role as a new Supreme Court Justice in the United States, it dovetailed into a movement that had started years before with women of color and picked up steam with the charges against the movie producer Harvey Weinstein in 2017 and was a long time coming: women collectively coming forward about the many ways we'd been abused and then silenced by power in our jobs, schools, churches, and families. The #MeToo hashtag catalyzed millions of posts and the #ChurchToo movement followed, with many people across gender identities bravely sharing stories of being sexually and spiritually abused—and silenced—by faith leaders in roles of authority.

In the work I do holding space for people who have been wounded by church and ministry, there's one universal thread that's weaved through every story—abuse of power by our leaders. I have friends who have been shunned by churches, removed from leadership positions, lost jobs, and been called heretical and rebellious for calling out unhealthy power (even though they attempted it in the most benign of ways). I also connect with people who have been emotionally and sexually abused by people in a position of power, both in and outside of church. I am in both categories as a survivor of church leadership abuse and sexual abuse as a teenager by a work supervisor; one thing I'm clear on is how truly harmful abuse of power is on our hearts, minds, bodies, and souls. It affects far more than we often initially recognize. I have tended to minimize pain, maximize shame, and not trust myself.

When the people who represent God, our churches, families, and organizations use power to harm in both subtle and overt ways, it messes with us. It can harm our psyche, make us leery of power, or sometimes remain drawn to authoritarian leadership, hoping we can find someone or something that will tell us what to do or think because that's what we're used to.

My heart aches for all of us who have been abused by power.

While we may sometimes feel alone in our stories, we're definitely not. We're alongside countless others across life experiences who are trying to find hope and healing after being abused by power. I'm personally grateful for the ways Jesus was continually calling out those who abused others with power, primarily religious power. Our hurt is not unfounded.

I discovered that the first step is to remember that abuse in any form is a trauma that needs to be acknowledged. *When people in positions of power and authority violate us, it is not a flesh wound—it's a soul wound.*

The way out is to grieve what's happened to us instead of stuff it down and blame ourselves. And the way out is to allow ourselves to be angry and lament the damage it's done to us in safe spaces, with safe people. We need to tell our stories and to do all we can to ensure that others aren't abused by power too.

If you've been abused by power, honor your pain today.
It hurts for a reason.

WEDNESDAY

Humility Not Shame

"Shame is a false sense of control."

—Katie Asmus[5]

Regardless of what we were taught in school or the false narratives that have been perpetuated, we now know that building the United States of America—the "land of the free"—required killing, relocating, and stealing land from the indigenous people who lived and prospered here for generations before. The ravages of colonization have created unjust societies across the globe that we continue to try to untangle from. Without deeper awareness of what really happened, we can't move forward.

At the same time, one of the most paralyzing factors in anti-oppression work is the shame that well-meaning people feel for sins of the past once the truth is revealed to us. I know this feeling well, and it's a powerless and limiting one. Shame is an incredibly potent factor in conversations about power. Shame can manifest itself in self-focused and paralyzing beliefs: *I'm ashamed of being white. I don't want to say the wrong thing. I'm afraid to do the wrong thing. I am all of the problem.* There are many more, but they all provide a false sense of protection that keep the story centered on us and block us from acting and healing. Myisha T. Hill, a Black author and community educator, focuses a lot of her work on challenging white people to find spaces for healing so that we're not stuck in shame. She reminds us that "the practices of liberation and learning are not rooted in shame. In fact, it is shame that keeps us prisoner to analysis paralysis that can plague our journey."[6]

If we are stuck believing that shame is the guiding response to the sins of our history, we will become immobilized (which is the exact opposite of what's needed to heal and repair these oppressive systemic patterns). My therapist, who saved my life after our son died, shared one of the most powerful truths I could have ever received as I wrestled with the shame of having a child who took his own life. She shared that "shame is a false sense of control." *Shame is a false sense of control.* Staying stuck in shame keeps us from feeling the grief that's underneath. It protects us in a damaging way that is the easiest to default to. If we are stuck in shame, we can never really heal or find our way forward.

The Lenten season is about breaking down defenses and changing our posture from self-protection to honest reflection and humility. If, as people who are on the upside of power, we constantly feel ashamed of our history or are always on the defensive, claiming that other people are shaming us, we will not be able to participate in healing. In the land acknowledgment we read at our outdoor gatherings at #beautyheals, which is a community retreat house and property that's part of a nonprofit organized by my husband and me, there's a line that sticks out every time we read it: "While we cannot change past history, we can participate in a better future through awareness, education, repentance, and reparations. *Humility, not shame, is the path of healing.*"

When it comes to untangling ourselves from our painful history, a perpetual cycle of shame keeps us in control and prevents us from the deeper work of grief. Humility, not shame, is the path forward.

How has shame kept you stuck?

THURSDAY

How Did I Not Know?

> "I need a love that is troubled by injustice. A love that is
> provoked to anger when Black folks, including our chil-
> dren, lie dead in the streets. A love that can no longer be
> concerned with tone because it is concerned with life. A
> love that has no tolerance for hate, no excuses for racist
> decisions, no contentment in the status quo. I need a
> love that is fierce in its resilience and sacrifice. I need a
> love that chooses justice."
>
> —Austin Channing Brown[7]

Years ago, I attended a multifaith Black Lives Matter vigil
in downtown Denver at a Black church deeply dedicated
to justice in our community. As I sat in the pews alongside
my husband, twin teenage sons, and a wide range of faith
leaders, I felt a painful reality deep in my bones: I realized
how little I knew about the experience of Black people in
our community. As a pastor leading an eclectic community
with people across a wide range of economic demographics,
I prided myself on being dedicated to equity.

Yet, a great chasm was revealed between what *I thought I
knew* and what *I actually knew*.

In 2022, our multifaith group traveled to Montgomery,
Alabama, for a three-day pilgrimage and learning trip to engage
with the ravages of slavery and mass incarceration in our country's history. It was soul stirring, to say the least, and a common
thread that emerged for all of us who were white, across faiths,
was how much we truly didn't know—what we weren't taught,
didn't learn, and were completely unaware of.

The prevailing comment was "How did I not know this?"

As we engage with lament this week, instead of beating
ourselves up with "What's wrong with us for not knowing
this?" (a shame response that can keep us paralyzed), we can

come to the table with a posture of humility and honest lament *that somehow we just didn't know.*

I grieve that I just didn't know. My privilege, faith, and culture I lived in protected me from knowing; and for that, I lament.

But now I do know more than I knew before, and each day I hope my ongoing learning increases. Now, we as a culture know more than we knew before, and each day I hope our communal learning together increases.

As we processed earlier, we can't heal a wound we don't think exists. When we know the story, the wound, the reality, the magnitude of what oppressive power can do, it will shape and inform how we move forward, together. Knowledge alone means nothing; it's the actions that are catalyzed from that knowledge that matters.

It makes me think of the wise words of the late poet and activist Maya Angelou, "When we know better, we do better."[8]

When we know better, we do better.

Take a few minutes today to honor
what you do know now that you didn't before.

FRIDAY

Impact, Not Intentions

"Intent is what you wanted to do; impact is the reality of
your actions."
—Elizabeth Perry[9]

One of the most significant nuggets of truth we've learned
together at The Refuge has been the difference between
intentions and *impact* in relationship with each other. When
it comes to power, we might think we're not saying or doing
things that create power divides or harms our connection.
While our intentions may be good, often our impact is
experienced by others in a completely different way.

This happened to me recently when I was navigating a challenging conflict between two people in our community. My
intention was to help solve the problem quickly, but in my
rush toward resolution for the sake of peace, I didn't realize
how using my power this way was affecting other leaders
who were also connected to the situation. The impact of my
actions were that they felt overlooked and that I hadn't considered other factors in the situation. They spoke up and told
me the truth. My first response was one of defensiveness, of
course! It's human to feel self-protective as a first response.
*Wait, I'm working so hard to try to help you, and now you're
mad at me for it?*

However, this is precisely what happens when we focus only
on our intentions—we think of ourselves first (and typically
stop there). We get tangled up in our own narrative and forget
that there are other perspectives and experiences completely
different from ours. Part of disrupting power is being willing to make changes based on feedback from people with less
power—the people who are being impacted.

In racial equity learning spaces, one of the most prevalent
themes I'm challenged by is that the good intentions of white
people, especially white women, are creating a negative impact

on people of color. We're so focused on doing good that we can't get our heads around how we might be doing harm. And instead of listening to constructive feedback, we often double down and remain entrenched in self-protection and defensiveness.

Real shifts in power and healing happen when we take time to listen to the impact we are having on others and use that crucial feedback to do better next time. It's extremely vulnerable, but it's also transformational. The reflex of defensiveness that often arises when we are repairing power dynamics is something to notice and acknowledge, remaining diligent to not let it blind us. My first response to hearing from my teammates needs to not be about me (intentions) but others (impact). As people on the upside of power, if we put ourselves at the center of the story, we are remiss. Plus, if we hide behind a self-protective covering of "Well, that's not what I meant" and ignore the possible impacts others are experiencing, we create harm in subtle and direct ways.

Impact matters more than intention.

Consider today how a good intention actually had a negative impact on someone else.

SATURDAY

Pause and Ponder: What Are We Lamenting?

As we engage with power, we are all entering from different places. Some of us are on the topside of power and privilege while others are on the underside, having felt harm in our lives, faith, and experiences. Most of us are probably some combination of both! Whenever I talk about grief, I always focus on the importance of remembering that "grief has no rules." We all process differently, and there's not one right way to lament or grieve.

What matters the most is that we do lament and grieve— that we look underneath our own personal experiences, consider others' stories and world and church history, and recognize that a significant portion of Jesus' life and ministry was calling leaders not only to self-reflection but also to actual change, sacrifice, and a new way of being. Jesus modeled grief for broken systems and hardened hearts in Luke 13:34–35 as he lamented, "Jerusalem, Jerusalem, the city that kills the prophets and stones those who are sent to it! How often have I desired to gather your children together as a hen gathers her brood under her wings, and you were not willing!" When it comes to misused power, there's a lot to grieve. Our work is to look at ways power has harmed others and how we've been harmed by it, to maintain a posture of humility, not shame, and to honestly examine our impact on others, not just our good intentions.

Integrating lament is lifetime work that propels us toward change. It's not an endless cycle of tears or handwringing, *I didn't mean to or I had no idea and I'm so dumb for not knowing*. It's sincerely looking at how our own power and powerful systems have impacted others and moving that awareness into action, where we turn from what is not healthy and toward a better way. That's where we're going next as we practice repentance related to power—*turning away from things that harm and divide and toward those that heal and repair.*

Wrestle, Reflect, Engage

Reflection Questions

1. As you look back on this week, what are some takeaways that emerged for you—words, phrases, feelings, ideas?
2. What are you lamenting as you consider these reflections? I grieve for _____. I lament _____. I am so sad that I didn't know _____.
3. How has shame paralyzed you when it comes to engaging with hard conversations about power and anti-oppression efforts?
4. When was a time that you had good intent but your impact harmed someone?

Prompts for Grief and Gratitude

- When it comes to power, I acknowledge that I have _____ or have not _____.
- I'm thankful that learning to grieve and lament is helping me _____.

Actions and Practices

1. Allow yourself to engage with world news from a trusted source, even when you want to ignore it. What do you lament? Where do you feel powerless? What do you want to look away from? How can you keep your gaze on it for longer and consider how power is at play in the story?
2. Make some space to consider a short inventory that can help with a soulful scan about power: *Where have you been harmed by misused power? Where have you possibly harmed others through overpowering—in your family, workplace, faith spaces? How have you not stepped into your personal power out of fear?*

3. Read more about the history of the city, state, or neighborhood you live in—from the indigenous people who originally thrived there to at least the 1980s, especially through the lens of power, wealth, and control. Let it sink in.

> *God,*
> *teach me to lament,*
> *to see myself in the story,*
> *to see others in the story.*
> *Help us cultivate openness, not defensiveness;*
> *presence, not denial;*
> *humility, not shame.*
> *Amen.*

Week Three

REPENT

"Your words mean nothing when your actions are the complete opposite."

—Anonymous

Unfortunately, I have a lot of words from my former Christian experience that I am still allergic to. Words and phrases like "God's in control," "blessed," "our hope is in heaven," and "are they a believer?" all make me a little itchy. Even though I know the intent behind them isn't malicious, the impact they have on people can be detrimental, especially for people on the underside of power, those who are grieving deep losses, or people from other faith or no-faith streams. If we pick them all apart more intentionally, we discover that underneath these kinds of trite spiritual phrases are issues of power and control, superiority, and centering ourselves instead of others.

The word *repent* is a word that is possibly on some people's lists too (or maybe it's a helpful word that doesn't bother you at all). I think many of us have a strong negative reaction to it because of past experiences. It's quite possible that when you scanned this book's table of contents you felt a little (or big) cringe as you read the word *repent*. Is this going to be another one of those *you better do this or else* . . . moments?

A few years ago, I was walking the streets of Calgary while visiting a dear friend and we came upon a young, hip-looking, male pastor with tattoos, earrings, and a bright red bullhorn telling everyone they needed to repent or they would perish. It was a bit of a mind twist (and a caution not to stereotype), and it reminded me that the message of repentance has been terribly mis-taught. No wonder so many are allergic to it!

Yet, here I am, making a pitch for it this upcoming week together. Even though I, too, have an initial negative reaction to *repent*, because of its misuse not because of its original meaning.

The Hebrew word for repentance, *teshuvah*, comes from a verb meaning to *return*. In the Jewish tradition there are specific practices related to the time of *teshuvah* during the ten days between Rosh Hashanah and Yom Kippur to focus not only on personal feelings but on right actions that lead to life.[1] Repentance is much more than feeling sorrow or regret that may be part of our lament. It's not only about turning away from something wrong; it's also about turning toward what's right, toward God, toward a better path.

Though most translations of Matthew 3:8 use the word *repentance*, I love the way the Bible in Basic English interprets the verse: "Let your change of heart be seen in your works." In an embodied way, as truth is revealed to us, it stops us in our tracks. We pause and allow ourselves to feel the impact and let our hearts be changed. Then, instead of continuing down the same path, we physically and emotionally turn and walk a new direction.

Untangling from unhealthy power requires repentance, not just lament. We need to move the grief and soul-stirring that's been revealed to us into action, to move us away from what was and into what could be. It makes me think of when Jesus was calling the disciples in Matthew 16:24: he asked them to turn away from the lives they had been living, to pick up their cross—the highest symbol of humility and sacrifice—and follow him.

It was a big ask then. And it's a big ask now.

But it's a crucial step forward.

It's also important to acknowledge that this path of humility and change is not exclusive to followers of Jesus.

Progress in shifting power is made through people across different faith traditions, life experiences, cultures, and spaces and places with the same basic elements—*being moved to action through some kind of soul transformation.* In other words, Christians don't have the market cornered on repentance. And we should be grateful for that because real change to oppressive power systems is going to require all of us—across binaries, boundaries, and borders. I firmly believe that people and institutions dedicated to embodying the ways of Jesus should be leading the way in terms of collective liberation and greater equity because that was the center of Jesus' message. Unfortunately, the zeal, inclusion, and equity of the early church didn't last long, because the default to institutionalized power is always the path of least resistance no matter the system.

In the world today, there's a lot to turn away from when it comes to dysfunctional power. Because of our human tendency to minimize, generalize, rationalize, and avoid when it comes to intentionally shifting power, we need to be confronted with stories and realities that transform not only our hearts but our actions too.

A core challenge for us this week is to engage with how a lot of us have accepted things as *just the way things are and have always been* because we haven't had good models for something different. Others have been under theological teachings that either placed us over or under others or bypassed reality as a form of self-protection, using superfluous spiritual platitudes like "well, things will be made right in heaven" to let ourselves (and our churches) off the hook.

Most of us engaging with this material are doing so because we truly do want to change. We want to gather courage and tools to help us move away from what's safe and comfortable to build what's equitable and healthy for everyone.

We want to turn away from what was and help build what could be.

And while this desire is strong, we also might be afraid—afraid of losing something that kept us safe, afraid of making mistakes, afraid of the unknown, afraid of the consequences of our changes in the circles we live and move in. Lent is a season for honesty, and naming fears helps us. I love these words from the Buddhist teacher Thich Nhat Hanh: "Only by looking deeply into the nature of your fear can you find the way out."[2]

Let's acknowledge our fear and consider the statement John the Baptist shared in Matthew 3:2—"Repent, for the kingdom of heaven has come near"—through a new lens where a change of heart is seen in our actions and we see repentance not just as a one-and-done moment but ongoing work to create a different kind of reality together, where we learn how to turn away from things that limit and oppress and toward what's good, true, and more equitable—over, over, and over again.

MONDAY

From Peacekeeping to Peacemaking

"Blessed are the peacemakers, for they will be called children of God."

—Matthew 5:9

A lot of us were taught to *keep the peace* in our families, churches, workspaces—to not rock the boat, to not speak out, to not cause problems, or to not make waves. In my family, I was the consummate peacekeeper, always making sure to stay in everyone's good graces, maintain my role as the "good girl," and not create conflict. As an adult child of an alcoholic, these patterns of codependence run deep. Instead of freeing me from some of these unhealthy ways of living, they became even more cemented into my life and experience when I became a Christian. I was taught that anger was a sin, that my role as a wife and mother was to be meek and mild, and that any relational dissonance could be resolved with prayer and "giving it to God." In other words, I learned even more clearly how to *keep the peace.*

It wasn't until years later that I saw that my peacekeeping tendencies not only were unhealthy for me personally but also perpetuated dysfunction in my relationships and the groups and organizations I was part of. I wasn't bringing my true self to the table, and I also went along with patterns that violated my core values of mutuality, authenticity, equity, and connection.

Jesus calls us to peace*making*, not peace*keeping*.

To disrupt power, we will need to turn away from false teachings that promote avoiding conflict and maintaining the status quo. We will need to learn to live with disapproval and practice speaking more boldly and clearly on behalf of ourselves and others. We will need to become peacemakers, not peacekeepers.

I keep learning that peacemaking is lifetime work and far messier than peacekeeping in the short term but far healthier in the long term. It also takes ongoing practice. This past year I knew

I was keeping the peace in an important ministry relationship, pushing down honest feelings in order to maintain ease. I felt stuck and resentful. When I started to share more honestly, speak more clearly, and advocate for change more strongly, it did create more conflict initially. However, in the end, through community and being willing to disrupt the status quo, a more authentic solution emerged that is far more resonant for everyone.

Peacemakers are willing to engage in conflict and work together to find better solutions. Peacemakers aren't in a hurry to try to come up with a quick solution that won't bring real change. Peacemakers are able to hold their ground and core values while honoring others' opinions and experiences. Peacemakers see beyond the moment and can stay in for the long story of healing and change, trusting our identities aren't at risk even when dissonance remains.

As we consider disrupting power together, may we keep turning away from keeping the peace and more authentically and bravely engage in making it.

How has being a peacekeeper prevented you from making peace?

TUESDAY

From Over or Under to Beside

"If you have come here to help me, you are wasting your time. But if you have come because your liberation is bound up with mine, then let us work together."
—Lilla Watson[3]

I do a lot of tours at The Refuge Cafe for people interested in volunteering or partnering with us on behalf of people experiencing homelessness and without social safety nets. Every time I usually say the same thing about our core value of friendship first: "Most of us learned how to be over or under others but not beside each other, and that's what we're committed to here—but it's always harder." *Over* or *under* are default positions in most of our culture; there are those who are over others as leaders and authorities and those who are underneath, usually not by choice but by social realities. Most societies are built on over and under. It's baked into almost every church or religious system as well.

Some would say these positions are comforting and that we need them to create order in our world. Others rely on theology to uphold it, using passages like "For the husband is the head of the wife just as Christ is the head of the church" (Ephesians 5:23) as a mandate to wives being under their husbands (even though v. 21, just two verses above it, says to mutually submit to one another). Others, who aren't necessarily religious, establish hierarchies through their leadership positions, economic privilege, or abilities.

I feel passionately dedicated to the idea that *over* and *under* philosophies and practices are not only damaging and limiting but also keeping unhealthy power structures in place. I'm not talking about different roles and gifts, which I respect; rather, we need to examine how power differentials are perpetuated and cemented through limiting beliefs about being better or worse off than others, more or less important and valuable than others, stronger or weaker than others, and more or less in need than others.

Part of our work this week is to consider ways we've put ourselves in either of these set positions—*over or under others.* How has that limited you? How has that limited others?

There's another option that feels crucial for change and needs far more practicing, together, over the long story—*beside.* Living more freely alongside one another in all our strengths and weaknesses, our beautiful and messy, with all of who we are and all of who we are not is a central way to disrupt power.

To me, over and under control, bind, and limit; while beside embodies freedom for "those who are oppressed" who Jesus names in Luke 4:18 (quoting Isaiah 61:1). This kind of freedom comes from learning how to truly live beside one another in our shared work of liberation. Unfortunately, Jesus' radical hope has been sorely misused by people bearing his name; instead of offering freedom to the world, we perpetuate systems and cultures that constrict and disempower, that create *over* and *under* instead of *beside.*

Our work is to repent from it—bravely and counterculturally turning away from *over* and *under*, and humbly and creatively toward *beside.*

*How have you put yourself over
or under others in an unhealthy way?*

WEDNESDAY

From Comfortable to Uncomfortable

"Be comfortable being uncomfortable"
—Jared Escobar[4]

While many of our icons and images portrait Jesus as a "nice guy" with warm, welcoming eyes and open arms, the truth is Jesus was a rabble-rouser, pot-stirrer, truth-teller, and master of making leaders and institutions feel uncomfortable. While we're in the season of Lent here, the same contradictory theme is true in the Advent season, where images of neat and tidy manger scenes are everywhere we turn even though the real Christmas story is a jumbled mess of discomfort, disruption, and upside-down power.

Everything about Jesus was subversive this way, yet modern culture most often tries to clean him up and make our lives cleaner too. Typical power is extremely resistant to anything uncomfortable. It likes its retention of the status quo, its predictability, separation, the knowns, and the rules—both spoken and unspoken—that keep the wheels of power spinning around.

Control and fear live underneath worldly power.

Swirling around, not just in our heads but also in our bodies and souls, is a fear of what will happen if we give up our positions, jobs, way of life, beliefs, or what we've worked so hard to build—personally, professionally, and spiritually. We also often fear engaging with things that we know will challenge us to move into unknown foreign territory.

This is why every time there is any kind of push against power, systems resist it, shut it down, hunker down, strengthen the logical arguments, and remind everyone what we need to be afraid of and why power should be protected. What has been played out in the red/blue divide since the United States presidential election of 2016 couldn't be more reflective of this reality.

What's underneath all the division? Fear of losing control, comfort, power.

But the ways of Jesus were always about being *uncomfortable* not comfortable, which I think was one of the primary reasons the most marginalized were also most drawn to him while those in power were out to do everything they could to shut him down.

As a young person, I was originally drawn to Jesus because I identified with marginalized people on the fringes of what was most valued by culture. Raised by a single mom struggling to make financial ends meet, with a dad who was a lifelong alcoholic and with no faith structure in our family, I had a friend who invited me to vacation Bible school in elementary school. I remember reading the stories of Jesus, being captivated by how he always went to the margins—the least, the last, the lepers, the outcasts, the women, those who were somehow rejected by religious leaders and the culture of the time. The religious leaders were painfully uncomfortable with Jesus' audacity.

One hundred percent of the time, shifting power will mean turning away from what's comfortable toward what's uncomfortable—risking disapproval, expecting resistance, and practicing using our voices and actions to disrupt the status quo on behalf of change.

What are some ways you are stepping out
of what's comfortable into greater discomfort?

THURSDAY

From First to Last

"It cannot be denied that too often the weight of the Christian movement has been on the side of the strong and the powerful and against the weak and oppressed—this, despite the gospel."
—Howard Thurman[5]

Remember when we were in grade school and picked teams by going back and forth? The first kids chosen were always the ones who were the strongest or smartest while the last were not as valuable to the winning of the game or high enough on the food chain of the elementary school social strata? Can you remember what it was like standing against a wall waiting to be picked and all the discombobulated feelings that come with it—relief when we're picked first, fear that we'll be last, resignation when we are? Or if you were always the picker or the team leader, can you remember the relief that position gave you?

Oh, power shows up in all groups starting at such a young age! Subtly and directly these patterns continue to be weaved into our lives. Whether we were first or last then or now, one thing I now know is that the ways of the world (and often the playground and church) don't align with the ways of Jesus, who was a master at turning things upside down, disrupting the status quo, and shifting power on its head. He was the one eating at a Pharisee's house and supporting an unwelcome woman interrupting their gathering to pour perfume on his feet (Luke 7:36–50) and calling a despised tax collector out of a tree and inviting himself to dinner (Luke 19:1–10).

As we consider repentance this week, for those of us who come from the upside of power, we can consider ways our unhealthy attachment to trying to be first has not only harmed us but others. I see myself in this part of the story as someone who likes to be the brightest and best and for years falsely bought into the idea that if people worked hard enough, anyone could get anywhere they wanted to go.

For those on the underside of traditional power, maybe the work is looking at how our striving to survive in certain systems we were and still are in has created exhaustion and resentment. To make it, you've had to adapt to things you never should have needed to.

Sometimes we fall into both categories at the same time. While I'm white, as a female Christian leader with over twenty years of experience bumping up against patriarchal systems, I do know a taste of what exhaustion and resentment feels like to try to get to higher places of leadership.

No matter which angle we're coming at this from, it's confusing for a reason. We get mixed messages all the time about who and what is more valuable—from evolving culture, terrible politics, and dysfunctional religious systems—and don't know quite what to do with it so we internalize it.

What if we let go of allowing a dysfunctional system to define who's first and who's last, perpetuating the same patterns we learned in elementary school? What if we, in the words of Howard Thurman, turn away from being on the "side of the strong and powerful" and toward "the weak and oppressed"? What if we stop ranking and evaluating one another, turn away from binaries and boxes, and expand our borders to see the beauty and contributions of everyone—including ourselves?

How has striving to be first, the best,
the strongest harmed not only you but others too?

FRIDAY

From the Sidelines to the Center

"The true measure of our character is how we treat the poor, the disfavored, the accused, the incarcerated, and the condemned."

—Bryan Stevenson[6]

Years ago, when The Refuge was starting, some people dreamed of it being a place where those who left megachurch-style Christianity with us would get some of what they were used to (teaching, worship, kids program) only in a smaller dose, with more real community. They didn't realize we were completely letting go of focusing our work on those three things. (We even explicitly said "We don't want people to come to The Refuge for the teaching, music, or kids' program—we want everyone to come for community.") It's not that those things have no value at all; it's just that from our perspective, when you center on them, you attract a certain kind of person—the kind that is typically the focus of most white Protestant churches, those who are financially resourced, educated, and family focused.

We had many church planters and local leaders coaching us with attractional culture practices like *you need to find the strongest leaders in your network and build The Refuge around them as your core or you'll fail.*

We ignored them.

It's one of the things I'm relieved we never got sucked into, even though we were tempted. We stayed the course because where would such a power block of leaders leave our friends who were single moms, people of all ages struggling with mental illness and physical disabilities, those recovering from and in active addiction, people who were experiencing homelessness, or our LGBTQ+ friends?

There's no question that it would leave them on the sidelines, not in the center.

I believe the wider church needs to repent from centering financially resourced people and courageously turn toward centering people typically on the margins. Full stop. Of course it has risks, liabilities, and consequences because it disrupts the dominant system and because people who are accustomed to being centered don't like being decentered. But isn't that what the wild ways of Jesus were always about?

The story of the "sinful" woman who busted into Simon the Pharisee's house while Jesus was eating there in Luke 7:36–38 comes to mind today. While outside of that room she existed on the sidelines, Jesus put her in the center, clearly chastising the religious leaders who rebuked her.

I know the feeling of the Pharisees well. In my early church years, I loved being the center too. I wanted what worked for me, my family, and my friends who looked, believed, and thought like me; I valued being apart from anything outside of my conservative Christian bubble. Thankfully, the bubble popped several years later, and when I entered a recovery community twenty years ago, I more clearly experienced what it looked and felt like when those typically on the sidelines are centered and when the poor, disfavored, accused, incarcerated, and condemned are our leaders, our teachers, our guides.

It's magical. It's wild. It's uncomfortable.

It's the kingdom of God come near.

It's *teshuvah*, repair.

What does centering others look like for you in this season?

SATURDAY

Pause and Ponder: What Can We Keep Turning Toward?

As we engaged with repentance this week, hopefully through a little different lens, I am wondering where you saw yourself in some of these stories? What caused you to constrict or feel defensive? What may have stirred your heart in a way it needed? I could feel in my own story how strong the pull always has been toward control, comfort, over and under, hierarchy, and centering on the most powerful instead of the least. And even though I deeply value the path of disrupting power, there are places in my heart and experience that still resist it, that don't want to turn away from it because it's far easier to maintain the status quo when the status quo benefits me.

This is why I love remembering that none of this work is ever complete but rather is always evolving. We will need to turn away from unhealthy power and toward what's better over and over for the rest of our time on earth. We will stumble and bumble. We will be drawn back to what feels safer and more comfortable. We will not perfect shifting power, but hopefully we'll continue to grow in openness and humility, have eyes to see disparate power patterns more clearly, integrate lament into our lives that leads to repentance, and turn away from what divides and harms and toward what ultimately heals and restores.

Healing and restoration don't come cheap or easy because power dynamics are so multifaceted. They come through disruption, conflict, dissonance, and hard work, together. That's what we're going to wrestle with next week.

Wrestle, Reflect, Engage

Reflection Questions

1. How do you connect with the action of repentance related to issues of power? What are you trying to turn away from and turn toward instead?
2. Wrestle with the idea of the default positions culture has taught us—that we're over or under others and rarely learn how to be beside. How has this showed up in your life? Can you see different parts of your experiences where you were in either of these positions? How did it affect you?
3. Share some ways you are learning to be "comfortable being uncomfortable." What is it feeling like for you? How is it transforming you?
4. What else emerged for you this week that you want to remember, consider, process?

Prompts for Grief and Gratitude

~ God, I acknowledge that my need to maintain control and the status quo has harmed _____.

~ I grieve how I have centered _____ instead of _____.

~ I am grateful for these specific people who have helped challenge my beliefs about power _____.

Actions and Practices

1. Make some space for an embodied practice that's simple and can help with releasing control. Get in a comfortable position and take a few deep breaths. Now clench your fists as tightly as you can. Take a few deep breaths. Next, slowly, intentionally, one small movement at a time, release your clenched fist and turn your palms up until your hands are open,

releasing, receiving. Do it several times slowly and intentionally. What does that feel like?

2. What's a group gathering, learning experience, cross-cultural faith community, or local collective action you have considered attending but know it will feel uncomfortable? Make a plan to go. Live with the discomfort and notice how it feels and what you're learning through it.

3. If you have been made aware of a way that you have perpetuated disparate power in your circle of work, family, friends, or faith, consider acknowledging it in some tangible way by sharing it with a trusted person or—if it won't harm you or others—make amends directly.

God,
help me move from control to release,
to become comfortable being uncomfortable,
to turn away from what harms and divides,
and toward what heals and repairs—
again, again, and again.
Amen.

Week Four

DISRUPT

"I am no longer accepting the things I cannot change. I am changing the things I cannot accept."
—Angela Davis[1]

That's just a little too much for people. These words were shared with me by an elder at the large, resourced church I worked for before The Refuge in response to our care team's challenge to center our work on the most marginalized in our community instead of those who were businesspeople and intact families. Our dream was primarily this: What if single moms, people struggling financially, our friends who were battling addictions, and people usually on the margins of churches were actually the center here? Yeah, it didn't go down so well. I got a pat on the head and a "that's just a little too much for people," and absolutely nothing changed. That's why we started The Refuge.

We could no longer accept the things we couldn't change and decided to change the things we couldn't accept.

Fear of change, concern about losing money, and self-protection for those who currently hold the most power keeps so many churches, ministries, and organizations from changing. In 2011, I wrote a book called *Down We Go: Living into the Wild Ways of Jesus* that was centered on practices that helped individuals and communities embody a life of descent—into problems and pain of real life—instead of a focus on ascent that many of us were taught where the goal was to rise above our problems and pain because of our faith in God. Downward mobility, on the whole, is not popular, especially in modern Christian culture that has mirrored popular culture where bigger is perceived as better, fast and efficient are valued, and ease is the goal. Most of us have been taught that moving up in the world is the path we should be moving on, not down. Yet, downward mobility is exactly the direction Jesus was pointing us.

A life of descent—which is centered on embodying the Beatitudes and leveling unequal power—is a disruptive one. Jesus upset the social norms by continually deferring to the margins and boldly confronting toxic religiosity.

The only way to shift power is to disrupt it and more bravely embody something different; to refuse to keep doing it the way we've always been doing it; and to risk being considered a heretic, rebel, or backslider to hold true to your values. This is what culture is experiencing now with millions of people leaving church each year, dissatisfied with the status quo.

A practical definition of *heretic* is "a person holding an opinion at odds with what is generally accepted."[2] In church history, heretics were burned at the stake. In my work with people who are shaking up power, challenging deeply rooted theological constructs and existing church systems, many have been called heretical (and much worse, trust me). I consider it a compliment because it means we are at odds with what is generally accepted.

When it comes to power, I want to be at odds with what is generally accepted.

A call to followers of Jesus to share power, lead the way on equity, and flip the script to decenter the most resourced and religious should not be considered bizarre, unattainable, or lofty. It should be what we do! I used to view The Refuge that way—that we were somehow the eccentric ones. But then I started to more boldly own that the domesticated, hierarchical, power-centered church system is what should be considered foolish, not us.

We need to reframe our understanding of norms that we consider off-kilter and identify existing power structures as wrong—not the desire for inclusion, equity, and shared resources. That should be the center of all we do as we follow the wild ways of Jesus.

And yes, that's disruptive—not because we're so innovative but because the current systems are so antiquated and oppressive.

Jesus made it very clear that creating a new kind of reality will require a countercultural way of living. It will mean giving up what we have held dear, making ourselves incredibly vulnerable, and humbling ourselves. It will mean giving up our power, diffusing what we have so that those who don't typically have any will get some too. It will mean sharing instead of hoarding, stepping up and stepping back.

This week we're going to engage with disrupting power—embodying something different from the current culture and taking the hits that come with rocking the boat. We'll consider ways we can break down divides, share power, lead, follow, and educate, agitate, and advocate for a different kind of reality in the circles we live and move in with actions and not just words.

It makes me think of the words of my friend Melvin Bray, who wrote the Truth and Transformation Model we engaged with briefly in week 2. Melvin always reminds us that "equity is a practice."[3] At a recent workshop for our Practicing Equity in Recovery group at The Refuge, he expanded on this with, "[Equity] is not an idea or a theory. It's not a conversation or a debate. It's not a sympathy or empathy that one expresses." Rather, "it's a story of human dignity that you can embody over and over, day after day, until it becomes a part of you and you become a part of it."[4]

Practicing equity is disruptive.

Telling the truth, leading, following, sharing, and getting into good trouble on behalf of change is disruptive—and that's why we need to keep bravely doing these things despite the costs.

MONDAY

Tell the Truth

"The heart of justice is truth telling, seeing ourselves and the world the way it is rather than the way we want it to be."
—bell hooks[5]

For some, disrupting comes easy. You're used to making waves and sharing truth to power. But a lot of us need some strength to do it—not only because it's hard to do but also because we haven't had practice because we weren't originally aware of these realities and are stepping into new territory. For those of us who feel the stir to disrupt current systems and break down our resistance to shifting power in our relationships, work, and faith, we need courage.

Brené Brown says that "Courage is a heart word."[6] She explains, "The root of the word *courage* is *cor*—the Latin word for heart. In one of its earliest forms, the word *courage* had a very different definition than it does today. Courage originally meant 'To speak one's mind by telling all one's heart.' Over time, this definition has changed, and, today, courage is more synonymous with being heroic."[7] She goes on to say that "I think we've lost touch with the idea that speaking honestly and openly about who we are, about what we're feeling, and about our experiences (good and bad) is the definition of courage. . . . Ordinary courage is about putting our vulnerability on the line. In today's world, that's pretty extraordinary."[8]

When considering ways to disrupt our current systems, it starts with ordinary courage: *speaking honestly and openly about who we are and about our experiences.* This can be sharing how we feel as friends, employees, leaders, or participants in programs, things we are observing or experiencing in the system that violate our values and we see as inequities. Ordinary courage means saying things instead of only thinking things and being an advocate for more equitable power, knowing that there are always risks associated with disruption. It's about telling the truth.

A few years ago, I had a conversation with a male ministry leader about my experience (and that of many other female leaders I know) when it came to patriarchy and the unaddressed power differentials that many of us observed in their church. I knew that speaking my truth directly would be risky, but I just couldn't pretend anymore. What I did share was simple and unemotional but also direct. As a result, it was the last time I got invited to coffee—ha!—or invited to lead anything at their community again. We sometimes lose our jobs, our positions or roles, or a host of other intangible things like respect, connection, and relationship when we stir the pot on power differentials instead of remaining quiet. However, it's the only way things will change.

I have found that the more I tell the truth about power, inequities, and the possibility for change, the less I am invited to play in certain circles I used to be part of. I have no doubt that a lot of people liked me better when I didn't speak up and speak out. The status quo is not wild about truth telling.

But that's exactly why we should do it.

Where do you need some courage to more freely tell the truth?

TUESDAY

Follow

"We don't come to the story entitled. We come to the doorway hungry, willing, and audacious. . . . We come humbly, with a good heart. We are learners here. Let's sit together in the back. There is so much we don't know."
—Idelette McVicker[9]

For those of us who are in positions of power and privilege, one of the most disruptive acts we can make is to humbly follow those who may not be in the dominant system, including Black, indigenous, and people of color, those who identify as LGBTQ+, and people with disabilities or without financial resources. The work is to not just listen to their stories but also actually do what they are challenging us to do. Many of us are open to learning, but to move that knowledge into action requires the humble act of following.

In the 2020 International Women's March to protest the policies and practices of the Trump administration, many of my friends and I were completely on board. We were guided by the desire to make our voice heard, stand in collective power, and show our support for not only gender equality but also all the additional ways progress was being threatened. While it was a very inspiring and impactful event, as I began following my Black and Brown friends' responses, I began to realize how I wasn't following their lead but rather following leadership that looked like me—white, resourced, and liberal, on the whole. Totally separate from my positive experience, many BIPOC leaders experienced woundedness from, once again, not being followed. It's a telling and painful mirror to gaze into and reflect upon.

Who are we actually following?

Are we following the same kinds of leaders who have typically held power, or are we following people whose power has often been diminished and can lead us in ways we need to be led?

When we started The Refuge, there were multiple people, including a core person on our leadership team, who weren't sure about following a female co-lead pastor. In their evangelical experience, they had been used to following only men in leadership. Honestly, a lot of people left when they realized I wasn't an assistant. They didn't want to follow. Many went back to a former church where there was outwardly strong and male-dominated leadership because that felt more comfortable.

Those who stayed and practiced something new were and still are participants in disrupting power. Now, almost two decades years later, The Refuge continues to be a place where we keep trying to follow people who usually don't get to lead.

My son Jamison is in his late twenties and works for a professional sports team as their first Diversity, Equity, and Inclusion coordinator. It's a tough job in a culture that thrives on hierarchical and celebrity-driven power and doesn't have a good reason to change because the status quo's been working just fine. Yet, it's exactly what they need to do—follow new, young, and diverse leaders who can bring the kind of disruption we need!

The disruption of power requires us to really ask ourselves, *who are we following*? For those of us who have typically held power, it's time to consider ways to follow others whose leadership has been missing. There's so much to learn and so many ways to grow and be challenged.

But we can't follow those others, won't follow those others, if we're always the ones leading.

Who do you need to follow and learn from more?

WEDNESDAY

Share

"It can seem so much simpler to ride solo, slaying your own dragons and singing the ballads you wrote about yourself. Collaboration can be tedious, and the prevailing masculine value system may have conditioned you to feel like you are giving away your power when you share it with others. So what? Give it away."

—Mirabai Starr[10]

Years ago, I led alongside a ministry leader that was not as interested in sharing power with people as I had hoped. There was fear involved in releasing the microphone and letting other people speak, share, and lead in some spaces of our community. I remember saying, "Our job is to give our power away as much as we can, however we can, and not keep it for ourselves because we've already had plenty of it," and his response was, "But they're not trained to do it, we are."

I know giving power away can feel scary, but it's a core practice to shift systems and embody something different.

A core piece of disrupting existing power structures is for those who are in leadership to learn what it means to diffuse power—to give away leadership, value, and voice as much as possible, as deeply as possible, as creatively as possible. While some people may think that diffusing evaporates power and spreads it out until it's no longer even apparent, diffusing and sharing power multiplies and expands power.

Giving away power is counterintuitive to what so many have been taught in terms of leadership. Early on in this journey we anchored in the simple truth that power is not finite like pie—instead, there's always more to go around. But another piece of power to name is that power is also attracted to power. This means that most of the time power is built by continuing to attract more of the same kind of power.

This looks like leaders replicating themselves and continuing to build and coalesce power instead of releasing it to those who aren't typically powerful—the marginalized, oppressed, the not-quite-as-pretty, talented, educated, and socially acceptable.

In the new reality that Jesus was always saying was possible, we all are important, we all have something to bring, we all have value, we all are uniquely powerful, and that's where liberation lives.

So how can we participate in sharing power, elevating others' leadership, value, and voice or stepping into our own? If we have it, find ways to share it, pass it on, give it to others, not just people like us. Give the microphone, platform, and leadership opportunities to others. Make more room at every table, keep pulling in more chairs and putting in more leaves. Fan people's passions into flame—find out what others love, care about, and believe in and support it. If we feel unempowered, find ways to gather support in community for the courage it takes to step into it.

Sharing power is disruptive, so let's share, share, and share some more.

What is holding you back
from sharing power in your circles?
Be honest.

THURSDAY

Practice

#keeppracticing

Much to my children's chagrin, I was always a mom who was a fan of "participation trophies" for any team sports or activity. Instead of always ranking the top 1, 2, and 3, honoring being in the game in any capacity is something to celebrate! Even though they are now in their twenties and thirties, they still tease me about this (and I still hold to it).

Disrupting traditional power systems is lifelong work, and to build a more equitable and healthy society we need everyone—typical leaders, untypical leaders, parents, singles, old, young. We all have a part to play. As many of us must participate, nobody wins because winning isn't the goal.

No matter our work, life, or faith realities, we all lead in different spaces. We all can utilize our different forms of power creatively. We all have families, jobs, groups, and communities where we have influence and possibility.

Disrupting power means we'll have to step into leadership in fresh, innovative ways, embracing our unique place in the story and remembering it won't come from thinking about it, reading about it, or listening to podcasts about it. To really shift power and work toward freedom and equity for all people, *we will have to tangibly practice it.* We're going to have to engage with our hands, feet, eyes, and ears, not just our heads. Practice comes from participation, not to win but to infuse something different in a world that won't change without us changing it.

What does practice and participation look like? It can be noticing power differentials in the groups and organizations we are part of, bringing conversations about it into the light instead of keeping it underneath the surface, using our positions to shift power by giving it away. It can look like helping others discover power is not like pie, and there's plenty to go around; and using our voices to advocate for healing and repair in our families, schools, communities, and faith spaces. It's stepping into our own power even when we are afraid.

We can't expect change overnight, and we can't change anything if we don't do something. Practicing, participating, and engaging disrupts. Bryan Stevenson, founder of the Equal Justice Institute, reminds us, "Somebody has to stand when other people are sitting. Somebody has to speak when other people are quiet."[11]

Let's be that somebody.

While there's always a cost to disrupting power, it's worth paying. Jesus reminds us of this in his power-disrupting Sermon on the Mount: "Blessed are those who are persecuted for the sake of righteousness, for theirs is the kingdom of heaven" (Matthew 5:10).

What is an area of your life you need
to more intentionally practice shifting power?

FRIDAY

Good Trouble

> "Get into trouble, good trouble, and most of all don't get lost in a sea of despair."
>
> —John Lewis[12]

A few years ago, I finally watched the *Good Trouble* documentary about the late John Lewis—congressman, activist, and person of faith deeply dedicated to the principles of nonviolence and a disruptor of power until his death in 2020. It is an inspiring story of how faith is moved into action over a lifetime (and painful, too, to see how much resistance there is to equality in our country). From the civil rights movement to leading during the tumultuous tenure of Donald Trump's presidency, John Lewis remained steadfast that we needed to keep on keeping on when it came to disrupting power and that all of us were needed—not only a certain kind of person or a certain kind of leader.

All of us need to make trouble, good trouble.

The National Voting Rights Museum in Selma, Alabama, is dedicated to telling the stories of the "foot soldiers" of the civil rights movement, those ordinary people of all ages, shapes, and sizes who usually weren't in the photographs like those leading the marches but were the powerful, united, and committed force of good troublemakers that turned the tide.

John Lewis also echoed the importance of not getting "lost in a sea of despair" as we witnessed how slowly the wheels of change turn, how hard it is to dismantle deeply entrenched power systems that are bent against diversity and equity. It can be discouraging, and I can't count the number of times the phrase "it sometimes feels hopeless" comes up in conversations about the current power divide in the United States, which feels like we are moving backward instead of forward, with a re-rising of nationalism and the fear-based movement against equity, diversity, and shared power in our world. It can be brutally discouraging.

But we have heroes of faith and justice movements who continue to inspire us to keep risking our egos and comfort to create a better reality, together. This will come only from getting into good trouble—speaking up, showing up, advocating, agitating, educating, practicing, and refusing to maintain the status quo that we know always holds unhealthy power in place.

Some ways we can get into good trouble are to follow good troublemakers, speak up and speak out, share power even when people are against it, and educate people with stories and resources. We can also advocate for change with our voices, our votes, our money and agitate the status quo by asking questions, challenging power, and mobilizing other people.

Are you getting into good trouble in this season of your story, or are you trying to lay low and stay out of trouble? Are you somehow working to shake up and mix up power structures in the spaces and places you live and work, or are you staying under the radar, trying not to rock the boat?

SATURDAY

Pause and Ponder: What Can You Disrupt?

As we finish this week together, I'm wondering what's stirring up in you as you consider being a disruptor of power in your unique spaces and places? In my bones the desire to disrupt resonates strongly with what I value and believe in, but I also experience a natural resistance to what's hard to do—truth telling, following instead of leading, sharing, practicing, and failing. But then I consider the inspiration and example of countless activists and community catalyzers who are committed to good trouble, to the long-haul commitment to shift power and create more equitable systems for everyone, to embody the ways of Jesus tangibly not theoretically, to rally alongside people of other faiths and perspectives for the greater good. This is why we must gain courage to tell the truth, to humbly follow, to share power in whatever ways we can, because, repeating the words of Melvin Bray, practicing equity is "a story of human dignity that you can embody over and over, day after day, until it becomes a part of you and you become a part of it."[13]

This work takes active cultivation, nurturing something healthier that changes the power structures, breaks down divides, and creates new possibilities for leadership and life that don't only change us but change the direction that power moves. That's what we'll explore next week.

Wrestle, Reflect, Engage

Reflection Questions

1. What words, phrases, or ideas emerged for you this week as we explored disrupting power?

2. Reflect on some areas where you live, work, and worship. Where are you trying to bravely tell the truth about power? What has that been like for you?
3. Are there more diverse leaders you are intentionally trying to follow and listen to that are out of your typical circle? If so, what are you learning? How is your world expanding? If not, who can you look to for guidance?
4. What does *good trouble* mean to you? What is helping you not get "lost in a sea of despair" when it comes to the long painful work of shifting power?

Prompts for Grief and Gratitude

- ~ I acknowledge sometimes I don't tell the truth related to imbalanced power because I'm afraid of _____.
- ~ It's sometimes hard for me to lead or follow because I'm used to _____.
- ~ I am grateful for more experience practicing and participating in the areas of _____.

Actions and Practices

1. Ponder an area of inequity that you feel passionate about, and consider a clear move forward you could make in that area—speaking up at a meeting, sharing truthfully in a group, writing a letter, showing up at a city council meeting, joining a social action in your community, standing up for yourself instead of remaining quiet.
2. Reconsider the teams you are on. How diverse are they? Who's missing? Whose voices are not being heard? Bring this to light and take action to move change forward; building more balanced teams is a disruptive act.

3. Learn from other leaders who are cultivating equity and integrate their input. What are they learning? What has the cost been for them? What have the benefits been? What mistakes have they made along the way? What are some ideas they might have for your organization, church, or group? There are a lot of people who have been doing this for a while and are glad to share their experience and encouragement.
4. Follow BIPOC, LGBTQ+, disability and economic justice activists, and community organizers on social media and commit to learn from them.

God, help us bravely
tell the truth,
follow,
share,
practice,
get into good trouble that disrupts,
that writes a better story, together.
Amen.

Week Five

CULTIVATE

"In today's America, we tend to think of healing as
something binary: either we're broken or we're healed
from that brokenness. But that's not how healing
operates, and it's almost never how human growth
works. More often, healing and growth take place on
a continuum, with innumerable points between utter
brokenness and total health."

—Resmaa Menakem[1]

While I personally have a black thumb and can't keep plants
alive for more than a few weeks, I have some friends who are
amazing organic farmers. They are patient, dedicated, and
focused when it comes to what is needed to grow cleaner
food. Because they don't create the straight and tidy rows that
are part of many commercialized farming methods, there's
often a false assumption about their work: that organic means
completely wild and untended and doesn't require much.
Really, it's the complete opposite. Growing this way, which
is countercultural, requires incredible intention, attention,
and collaboration.

The same is true for shifting power. It doesn't happen on its
own. It needs deep and faithful cultivation. It requires patience
and resolve. When you think of the word *cultivate*, what comes
to mind? For me, it resonates with actions like nurturing, catalyzing, supporting, empowering, growing, tending. When it
comes to cultivating healthy power, we have a lot of work to
do. Without intentional nurturing, catalyzing, supporting,
empowering, growing, and tending, we will always default
back to what was; in the often-paraphrased words attributed

to Albert Einstein, *the same minds that got us into the problem can't get us out.*

We can't change the past, but we can openly acknowledge our true history. We can't go back in time and become someone we're not, but we can do better now, equipped with greater knowledge and healing. We can't rely on the same minds that got us into the problem, but we can get new minds in the room and follow them.

The solution is not "out there" somewhere at the next cool conference, in the newest book, or in a best-selling program. It's available now, in us, around us, through us—in people of color, LGBTQ+, immigrants, refugees, women, people who live in poverty and on the margins, youth, voices we've never heard, the wisdom of other faith traditions, and people who want to learn to share power instead of hoard it. Thankfully, they have the minds, ideas, hearts, passion, imagination, and practices to get us out of this mess and help us all cultivate a better future.

This kind of collaborative power is what needs to be cultivated, tended to, nurtured, expanded. In the parables, Jesus used metaphors and imagery of seeds, soil, yeast, and trees in different places in the Gospels to teach a variety of lessons. The parable of the Sower comes to mind as we consider creating good soil that can produce healthy, cooperative power, together. Matthew 13:1–9 reads like this:

> That same day Jesus went out of the house and sat beside the sea. . . . And he told them many things in parables, saying: "Listen! A sower went out to sow. And as he sowed, some seeds fell on a path, and the birds came and ate them up. Other seeds fell on rocky ground, where they did not have much soil, and they sprang up quickly, since they had no depth of soil. But when the sun rose, they were scorched, and since they had no root, they withered away. Other seeds fell among thorns, and the thorns grew up and choked them. Other seeds fell on good soil and brought forth grain, some a hundredfold, some sixty, some thirty. If you have ears, hear!"

When I'm reading the Bible, I often like to add synonyms to expand practical applications to the existing words and highlight contextual truths. It can help us create new interpretations that inspire and challenge. For me, when I shift "the word" or "the word of the kingdom" to "truth about power" instead, I feel a stronger connection to the importance of honestly engaging with power and cultivating something different. Here is Matthew 13:18–23 with this shift:

> "Here then, the parable of the sower. When anyone hears the word of the kingdom [i.e. the truth about power] and does not understand it, the evil one comes and snatches away what was sown in their heart; this is what was sown on the path. As for what was sown on rocky ground, this is the one who hears [the truth about power] and immediately receives it with joy, yet such a person has no root but endures only for a while, and when trouble or persecution arises on account of [the truth about power], that person immediately falls away. As for what was sown among thorns, this is one who hears [the truth about power], but the cares of this age and the lure of wealth choke the [truth about power], and it yields nothing. But as for what was sown on good soil, this is the one who hears [the truth about power] and understands it, who indeed bears fruit and yields in one case a hundredfold, in another sixty, in another thirty."

"But as for what was sown on good soil, this is the one who hears the truth about power and understands it, who indeed bears fruit. . . ." This is the one who cultivates healing, repair, change, possibility, who creates a new reality, the kingdom of God that is contrary to the kind of "kingdoms" we're used to. This is what I want to do with my time on earth—be a cultivator of healing, repair, change, and possibility, a participant in creating a new reality, alongside whoever else is in on it too.

We don't have to have all the ins and outs of power figured out; we don't have to be completely schooled in world or church history; we don't have to have a certain role, position, or vocation to be part of cultivating healthier power in ourselves and the systems we're part of. What we need is a willingness to be open, to remove the blinders from our eyes, to grieve ways we've harmed and been harmed, to turn away from what divides and separates and to what supports and heals, courage to disrupt the status quo, and a desire to cultivate the good soil of collaborative power, together. These postures are like tiny mustard seeds that can move mountains.

This week we're going to explore ways we can keep tending, nurturing, growing, catalyzing, and cultivating collective power together, starting with three *w*'s I find very meaningful: *with*, *wisdom*, and *webs*. These are part of the continuum that holds our path between brokenness and wholeness. They are the good soil that can help the seeds we plant grow to trees that bear new fruit this world desperately needs. They are about practicing new ways of being that lead to life and reflect healthier power.

MONDAY

With

"Our work is to call each other home, to call to one another's spirits and say, 'This is for you. This is what it means to be human, to love and be loved. Let's learn from one another as we go.'"
—Kaitlin B. Curtice[2]

A guiding preposition in the life of The Refuge is *with*. Although it's very hard to do, we try to avoid doing things *to* or *for* others, which are the typical set positions of a lot of ministries and programs. Doing things *to* others is paternalistic and has created abusive power dynamics in many systems. It fosters dominance and creates oppression; it is the basis of colonization. *For* is a little less dominant but also fosters unequal power because we do things *for* others, which often implies we're somehow better, know more, have more; it's maternalistic and can create codependence.

Both *to* and *for* protect power and leave whoever and whatever's on the underside of it in a position of less-than.

With shifts that.

It's an alongside posture, both giving and receiving, a shared humanity, a shared experience. *With* is incarnational and creates transformation, freedom, and healing. It is what Jesus embodied. *With* is also a lot harder to live out! It's far more vulnerable, raw, and messy. But that's where the transformation we need comes from.

Researcher, author, and storyteller Brené Brown reminds us that while *power over* stems from fear, daring and transformative leaders (which we all are, in our different contexts) share power *with* others, which strengthens people to live out healthier practices, and inspires people to develop power *within*.[3]

If we want to get to the root of power dynamics, we need to cultivate more *with: power with, life with, leadership with, love with, activism with, faith with, change with, healing with.*

With.

It's why no matter how much my faith has shifted, I haven't let go of the upside-down story of Jesus—Emmanuel, God *with* us—not doing things to us or for us, but with us. Alongside us, near us, beside us, in the thick of us.

Even though they are so much easier to live out, *to* and *for* keep the wheels of the empire spinning because they keep people over and under each other. *With* can seem harder, messier, and inefficient (things systemic power likes least), especially when we're not used to relating this way. However, healing and repair comes from resisting letting the path of least resistance guide our actions and opening ourselves to what's harder but better.

With might feel harder, but it's so much better.

How can you cultivate more with *in this season of your story?*

TUESDAY

Wisdom

"We need acts of restoration, not only for polluted waters and degraded lands, but also for our relationship to the world. We need to restore honor to the way we live, so that when we walk through the world we don't have to avert our eyes with shame, so that we can hold our heads up high and receive the respectful acknowledgment of the rest of the earth's beings."

—Robin Wall Kimmerer[4]

In most of Western culture, elders aren't valued in the same way as they are in indigenous and Black and Brown communities. Ageism is embedded into our society, and instead of gleaning from the profound wisdom and experience of seniors, we often dismiss their offerings and elevate youth and perceived beauty instead.

The indigenous community should be our guide on sharing power and cultivating wisdom. My friend is an Athabascan elder, serving in the community in the most beautiful of ways through presence, connection, and care for others. Embedded into their culture are circles instead of hierarchies, a slower pace instead of quick decisions, and honoring the wisdom of elders and youth, who often have so much to bring but are easily dismissed. Doug's presence is highly valued alongside other elders—not for what they can *do* or are *doing* but for the wisdom and experience they bring because of who they are. Also, watching the pace he works at—slow, steady, and seemingly inefficient—is always good for my soul.

It is beautiful. And, unfortunately, rare.

In our fast-paced, flashy culture that perpetuates unhealthy power, we have a lot to learn in this space. Robin Wall Kimmerer, who is Potawatomi and founder of the Center for Native Peoples and the Environment reminds us, "Leadership is rooted not in power and authority, but in service and wisdom."[5]

There are tangible ways to cultivate more service and wisdom.

No matter our education, background, experience, bank account, role, or position, how can we more deeply value and learn from the wisdom of elders in our family, faith community, workspace, finding ways to connect, learn, travel *with*? If we are older, how can we not diminish our gifts and think we're past our prime, with nothing to contribute, and find ways to be of service, to be part of multigenerational, active, and rooted communities that honor our contributions?

To shift power and nurture healthier groups and families, we need to cultivate these crucial relationships and grow our roots into the rich, fortifying soul of wisdom.

Who are some wise voices in your life
that challenge you to healthier power?

WEDNESDAY

Webs

"Revolutions do not happen only in grand moments in public view but also in small pockets of people coming together to inhabit a new way of being. We birth the beloved community by *becoming* the beloved community."

—Valarie Kaur[6]

Imagine a world where the imagery that most dominates our society is one of webs, not ladders, an interconnectedness without rigid hierarchies and walls of separation, a weaving of people and communities that are symbiotically connected to one another. I believe this is the "earth as it is in heaven" that Jesus shared was possible, now.

And it's up to us to create it.

A few years ago, my friend Jen and I were on a beautiful fall walk with our dogs, talking about our desire to have more feminine wisdom weaved into the power structures of all our systems and organizations. She's a former pastor and community dreamer, and we talked about the need to bring women together in webs of support so that we could not only last but also thrive in our toxic cultures. This was the birth of a small, organic, nonhierarchical collaboration we loosely call the Web of Wise Women. We don't have a website, program, or leadership structure. What we have is shared values of inclusivity, collaboration, support, and the wisdom of women. We gather in small, eclectic, and creative pockets in various ways, cultivating support and nurturing each other in our lives and work. I know as you're reading you might be asking, "But what about structure . . . leadership . . . process . . . ?" It's not that these things don't matter, but do you notice how we typically go to those places *first*, looking for a clear order of things that match the ways of the world? Breaking these natural reflexes is crucial to change.

The early church was a wild and scrappy web of relationships where resources were shared, and no one went without; however, because of hierarchy, power grabs, and arguments over theology, it eventually devolved into the thing it was created to subvert. Yet, even now, with our current culture's replication of the Roman Empire in full swing, there are still so many underground, small, grassroots organizations around the globe—clusters of passionate people committed to a better way, creating webs of hope and love even though the rich and powerful don't value them, donate to them, or even know they exist. It amazes me.

We need to cultivate more webs, and in the words of Sikh community activist and cultivator of love and wisdom, Valarie Kaur, more "small pockets of people coming together to inhabit a new way of being. We birth the beloved community by *becoming* the beloved community."

We need more webs and fewer ladders.

What are some webs you can cultivate?

THURSDAY

Living Systems

Shalom—שָׁלוֹם—completeness, soundness, welfare, peace
—Strong's Exhaustive Concordance[7]

My friend Pam Wilhelms Johnston is an organizational development consultant and executive coach and is passionate about cultivating healthier systems in all sectors of life, including business, government, and faith. Core to her work is the focus on moving away from traditional hierarchical systems to the ongoing cultivation of healthy, living systems that are more aligned with not only the ways of Jesus but the ways of the natural world.

When we're considering shifting power, systems matter. They are how we organize, how we get things done, and where we live. When we're talking about foundational shifts in our theology and practices related to power, we must consider systems. Traditional systems have carried us for years now—the industrial revolution, mechanization of labor, and hierarchical systems in all our sectors have brought order to our society in many ways. At a theology camp The Refuge hosted a decade ago, Pam shared how in this mechanistic worldview three methods permeate: *domination, pressure, force.*[8] These are strong words but accurately describe it.

These things had their place in our story but will not get us to a better future. The world is changing, and there's a collective wisdom that is growing that this domination model is leading us toward destruction not life, toward fragmentation not wholeness, toward violence not peace. There's a groaning, a desire, a longing for shalom, for peace, for us to "pour new wine into new wineskins" (Matthew 9:17 NIV) where structures change too.

Biblical shalom is about integrity, wholeness, togetherness, soundness. In community, I think it can mean a living system that speaks a living language centered on the opposite of dominate, pressure, and force, and what Pam calls us to consider—creating systems dedicated to the three actions of *nurture, cycle, grow.*[9]

Nurture means to tend to, to cultivate, to create the best environment for the right things to grow. Cycle is about recognizing that everything is always changing, moving, and evolving. Grow is about developing and transforming.

Living systems are about collaboration, partnership, and synergy. They are about diversity and the power of everyone's unique contributions, the process instead of only the outcomes, people and relationships instead of only programs, mutual submission and equality and valuing each other's differences, healing racial, political, and economic divides so that all can flourish, and integrity and wholeness and our true need for each other.

Isn't that what we want to create more of? Living systems so that all may flourish. Cultivating The Refuge community is one of my favorite things on the planet because we get to be part of reflecting what's possible in our little corner of the world—a system that's far from perfect but is trying to be a place where people who were used to being part of systems that pressed, dominated, and forced can now experience the values of nurture, cycle, grow in real life. This doesn't have to be an impossible task, and we don't create it overnight. As we move toward Holy Week, I hope we can consider how we can cultivate shalom-embodied living systems that reflect the kingdom of God here, now—places and spaces and pockets embedded in love, freedom, hope, justice, mercy, connection, collaboration, and equality in all kinds of creative ways.

How are you cultivating life in the places you live and move in?

FRIDAY

Creativity

"The essential ingredients for creativity remain exactly the same for everybody: courage, enchantment, permission, persistence, trust—and those elements are universally accessible. Which does not mean that creative living is always easy; it merely means that creative living is always possible."

—Elizabeth Gilbert[10]

Whenever I'm in a room talking about creativity, I often ask the same question: "How many of you in the room consider yourself an artist?" There are always a few people who raise their hands, but most shake their heads with "nope, not at all." Then I ask, "If you were in kindergarten, and I asked you that same question, how many of you would say yes?" Most of the time, all the hands shoot up!

We've got to get some of that imagination and courage back to cultivate a different kind of society together!

In this book, we're talking about power, not art, but the exact same principles apply. If a group of us were in a room together and I asked you, "How many of you play a role in shifting and disrupting power in this world?" my guess is that a few leaders would maybe cautiously raise their hands. Yet, the truth is all of us should be holding our hands boldly in the air. We all have a part to play and need a spirit of "courage, enchantment, permission, persistence, [and] trust," as Elizabeth Gilbert says, to move some possibilities for more power *with*, webs, wisdom, and living systems filled with shalom forward. We need to believe we all have our gifts to bring and remember "there are many parts, but one body. . . . Each one of you is a part of it" (1 Corinthians 12:20, 27 NIV).

Owning our own personal power and bringing it to the table is crucial. Together, all of us, across all our differences and unique contributions, we can create something different.

Reimagining what could be related to power requires creativity, innovation, practicing, and risk. Jesus' message was meant to be continually adapted and contextualized through people moved by the creative wind of the Spirit, willing to not just believe what is possible but cultivate it courageously, creatively.

What's your part to play?
What imagination can you bring to shifting power in your contexts?
What's your unique part of the body?

SATURDAY

Pause and Ponder: What Are You Cultivating?

As we wrap up this penultimate week of Lent and transition into Holy Week, I'm reminded how all these ideas about power are strongly intertwined. As we cultivate more with-ness, we can draw on more wisdom from our elders and youth through stories and experience, building webs of inclusion and support that catalyze healthier living systems that inspire and multiply creativity and imagination. Cultivating healthy power is cultivating "heaven on earth," where all can thrive and flourish, where divides between us are broken down, where the ways of the world are turned upside down, and where we experience the kind of shalom many people long for—greater *completeness, soundness, welfare, peace*. Walter Brueggemann, author of the timeless book *The Prophetic Imagination*, reminds us, "The task of prophetic ministry is to nurture, nourish, and evoke a consciousness and perception alternative to the consciousness and perception of the dominant culture around us."[11]

When it comes to power and the dream for a different reality, Holy Week illuminates it in the most simple and profound way that disrupts, transforms, heals, and inspires. It's a tangled mess of hope, confusion, challenge, death, grief, new life, and the desire for and resistance to a different kind of power. What was at play then is still at play today. All roads led to power then, and they still do. As we step into this last week together carrying our desire to disrupt and cultivate something different in this world, may we avoid trying to pull all the details about power together into a neat and tidy package, which is a futile exercise. Instead, may we live with power's complexity while finding simple but meaningful ways to transform it. That's what this week can teach us.

Wrestle, Reflect, Engage

Reflection Questions

1. What words, phrases, or ideas emerged for you this week?
2. How are you cultivating *with,* wisdom, and webs in the spaces and places you live and move in? What are you learning?
3. Consider the groups you are part of, where are you seeing a shift away from hierarchical systems to more living ones (or what are you dreaming it could be like)? What does that look and feel like?
4. Reflect on some of the essential ingredients for creativity that Elizabeth Gilbert names: "courage, enchantment, permission, persistence, trust." Which of these resonate as areas you want to develop for yourself, your family, the groups, and the organizations you are part of?

Prompts for Grief and Gratitude

~ As I acknowledge how many faith and professional spaces I've been part of that are centered on power *over*, not power *with*, I feel _____.

~ I give thanks for these people and ideas who embody and cultivate *with*, wisdom, and webs, challenging and inspiring me to _____.

Actions and Practices

1. If you are a leader in any context, consider engaging with Brené Brown's work of Power Over and Power With/To/Within available on her website.[12]
2. Set aside some time to intentionally connect with an elder in your family, workspace, or community. Ask

them to share what they are seeing or experiencing in the systemsthey are part of and what they wish we'd consider. Bonus points for doing the same with youth.

3. Draw, paint, sculpt, or make something that embodies your desire for living systems and greater shalom and what you envision or see or hope for.

God,
we want to be cultivators of peace, equity, and healing.
Teach us the power of with-ness;
show us how to draw on untapped wisdom
and create webs that include, empower, support, and inspire.
Spark our imaginations.
Give us courage to cultivate a new reality.
Amen.

Holy Week

ILLUMINATE

The next day, the news that Jesus was on the way to Jerusalem swept through the city. A large crowd of Passover
visitors took palm branches and went down the road to
meet him. They shouted,

"Praise God!
Blessings on the one who comes in the name of the LORD!
Hail to the King of Israel!"

Jesus found a young donkey and rode on it, fulfilling the
prophecy that said:

"Don't be afraid, people of Jerusalem.
Look, your King is coming,
    riding on a donkey's colt."
                                    —John 12:12–15 NLT

It's hard to believe that we are already here—Palm Sunday
and the entrance to Holy Week, making our final steps on
the road toward Easter. This story took place two thousand
years ago, yet the irony is that many of the exact same basic
human dynamics are still in motion today—only with more
technology and scarier global consequences. Empire continues to dominate and oppress, powerful structures and people
continue to resist sharing power, and the most marginalized
continue to live with the consequences. As we travel through
these upcoming days and the twists and turns in the story
through the lens of power, there's a lot to be illuminated.

Jesus starts this wild week entering Jerusalem to a roar of
"hosannas!" and the anticipation of a coming victory with him
riding on a simple donkey instead of a powerful horse. (I love
all the mixed-up imagery of every Jesus story.) People were
inspired and ready for a king, ready for Jesus to fulfill the scrip-
tural prophecy, to crush the empire and restore justice. They
had been overpowered and oppressed for too long, and it was
time for the tides to turn. They were ready for someone who
would finally make all that was wrong right. Little did they

know then that just a few short days later this king would die on a cross alongside other accused criminals.

The story of Palm Sunday shines a light on humanity's hope for a particular kind of power, a certain kind of king, queen, or powerful group that helps us get our way. Our intersection with putting our hope in a strong leader looks differently for each of us, but it likely exists because it's been ingrained in us through the complex entanglements of patriarchal systems and world history; these early followers of Jesus were just using the social framework they were used to.

But now, as we know better and have generations of examples of the same power-over story told over and over again (with the same results), I'm always struck by how popular certain authoritarian, hierarchical leaders have continued to be followed and revered and how complicit Christian systems are in the perpetuation of the elevation of "powerful kings" in leadership. I used to follow leaders like this too! In many years of my conservative faith, I loved certainty, charisma, someone to tell me what to believe or not believe, and an affiliation with a similar group of people. When I look back at it, I know it was centered on a desire for security and protection in a system that felt clear and certain after being raised in a family without a lot of boundaries and safety. I think a lot of our need to follow powerful leaders is somehow about our own survival and often even primal. The political landscape in the United States and abroad, the popularity of fear-mongering leaders who tell people their safety and survival is at risk, is painfully illuminated in this season of our society. Following certainty brings us security, othering brings us a group to belong to, and divisions secure our position.

However, the message of Jesus—what's supposed to be good news—isn't and was never supposed to be protected, comfortable, or contained. I always chuckle when I think of all the unkingly things Jesus did—gathering the most unqualified and unprofessional group of leaders, touching lepers, eating with outcasts, shaking down religious systems instead of buddying up to them, modeling inclusion instead of exclusion, promoting relationship instead of force.

Yeah, Jesus was definitely a different kind of king.

So why do we keep following the other kind?

It's OK to listen to thought leaders and glean what we can from them, to agree with values and practices of leaders and support them, to gather what inspiration we can in a world that feels full of despair right now. This Palm Sunday, as Jesus' countercultural power is illuminated, I'm just encouraging us to notice this phenomenon of hopping on bandwagons in our culture that lead us down a completely different path than we expected. To be careful about who we are following. To look at what we're getting out of being part of an amped-up crowd (or for some of us, being the cynical, skeptical one). To notice what we'll do to belong or somehow be part of the latest and greatest movement.

For the most part, we spend far too much time (and money!) listening to or following charismatic leaders instead of washing other people's feet, sacrificing our comfort, and following the example of Jesus, who often leads us places that don't always feel exciting, don't make sense, and certainly don't make us leave every encounter saying, "I feel so safe and protected."

This Palm Sunday, I hope we can shed false hope for something shimmery and over-spiritual and strip down to the bare, simple, and unplugged. That's where real power lies. There aren't many kings like that, but I'm pretty sure that's the one we are supposed to be following.

Look, a [different kind of] king is coming.

What do you need to consider about following "kings"?

MONDAY

Turning Over Tables in the Temple

"Healthy anger can be our friend"
— Jeff Jernigan[1]

The next thing Jesus did after he entered Jerusalem on a donkey
to the cheers of "hosanna!" was go straight to the temple and
start turning over tables:

> Jesus entered the Temple and began to drive out all the
> people buying and selling animals for sacrifice. He knocked
> over the tables of the money changers and the chairs
> of those selling doves. He said to them, "The Scriptures
> declare, 'My Temple will be called a house of prayer,' but
> you have turned it into a den of thieves!"
>
> The blind and the lame came to him in the Temple,
> and he healed them. The leading priests and the teachers
> of religious law saw these wonderful miracles and heard
> even the children in the Temple shouting, "Praise God for
> the Son of David."
>
> But the leaders were indignant." (Matthew 21:12–15 NLT)

Indignant. Some other words for it are *resentful, furious,
incensed, miffed, displeased, upset, boiling, bent out of shape.*
Even though this word was used to describe the leaders in the
moment, I think it aptly describes what Jesus was feeling too.
And what so many of us are experiencing these days, indignant
at the unholy marriage of faith to an ultraconservative political
agenda. *Resentful, furious, displeased, bent out of shape.*

We're wondering what to do with what we feel is a painful
hijacking of our faith. What do we do with the religiosity we've
seen choke out freedom for so many? What do we do with
the ways that the "system" of Christianity is tied to money,
power, resources, and separation from people's real needs?
What do we do about the dehumanization of the LGBTQ+
community, immigrants, and refugees that is fueled by many

faith leaders, along with Christian nationalism? What do we do with the big feelings of anger and embarrassment about the values that Christianity has become known for and how tangled up it's become in a particular political party? There's a lot of deep anger floating around about the money changers, law enforcers, and gatekeepers of the faith who have always held power, but something about the extra polarized political landscape and associations with faith coalitions has illuminated it more clearly.

Anger is hard for me because my family of origin and damaging theology taught me that it's a sin. Anger is not a sin. It's a propelling emotion. I love that Jesus' first act of Holy Week is to go straight to the place that thought it was doing right and expose it for what it was—*a system rigged against the poor, weak, vulnerable, desperate, broken, sick, oppressed.*

I'm not proposing we all do it the exact same way as Jesus, but I love the reminder that we're not offtrack in seeing that something's not right about our system and the injustice it often perpetuates, the bondage it often creates, and the legalism it often breeds. There's a lot to be mad about.

What are some tables you want to turn over right now?

TUESDAY

Unbinding Each Other

"We are caught in an inescapable network of mutuality, tied in a single garment of destiny. Whatever affects one directly, affects all indirectly."
—Reverend Dr. Martin Luther King Jr.[2]

Part of Jesus' big and busy week includes a story we find in John 11, in which Jesus says two simple words that are worth exploring today. After finding his way to his friend's house upon hearing that Lazarus had died, Jesus raises Lazarus from the dead and calls him forth. However, as Lazarus walks forward, alive again, his graveclothes didn't magically fall off him. Instead, in that strange and supernatural moment, Jesus turns toward his community, the dear friends in Lazarus's life, and tells them to "unbind him" (v. 44).

Unbind him.

Take off his graveclothes, together.

Instead of the instantaneous and miraculous healing we sometimes attribute only to Jesus, I love this simple twist in the story that I believe embodies what we often miss—the healing power of ongoing work in community together, to unbind our wounds, to set each other more free.

When it comes to the realities of unhealthy power in our lives, there's a lot to heal from and a lot of graveclothes to be removed. No matter our different angles, sides, and perspectives, stepping into new life and practices around power is not something that comes in an instant. We need help, support, ongoing healing, and accountability, and we can offer the same to others. Mutuality is one of the most transforming ingredients in shifting power.

The graveclothes we might be wearing related to power are different for all of us. Some might be the lies we've been told that we're better than or worse than others; others might be our fear and insecurity and how that causes us to control ourselves and others in unhealthy ways. Some might be centered around shame that keeps us paralyzed or destructive messages spinning around in our minds like *I'm not enough. I'm too much. I'm too damaged. I have to stay in control or else the world will fall apart. It's all up to me. I don't deserve anything good. What's the use? It's all hopeless anyway?* Or it might be rage we feel about unjust systems that keep us constricted and stuck.

No matter our realities, we need supportive community to unbind us, not once, not twice, but for the long story of unraveling from unhealthy power and finding our way to new life. We're all connected. We all need support.

Let's keep unbinding each other.

In this season of your story, who's unbinding you?
Who are you unbinding?

WEDNESDAY

Scapegoats

scapegoat: a person or group made to bear the blame for others or to suffer in their place.

—Dictionary.com[3]

On the journey toward Easter, we prepare for the biggest scapegoat in history: Jesus. We see what happens to a scapegoat. We see how the crowds turn in a snap. We see betrayal. We see the consequence of our sociological dysfunctions and human brokenness.

In conversations about power during Holy Week, we would be remiss to not reflect on scapegoating and how strongly it is at work today—in families, groups, organizations, almost any system we are in. René Girard, a French philosopher of social science, writes about this in his well-researched and utterly fascinating mimetic theory where he nails a critical point about human nature—*our tendency toward violence and scapegoating.*[4]

Violence doesn't always look like guns, bombs, and physical assault. Violence looks like turning against our brothers and sisters, ourselves, and even God to protect ourselves. This can come out in all kinds of different ways that are far more subtle than war. We separate, turn against, withdraw, blame, and point the finger—to protect ourselves, to save our own skin. Families, companies, churches, politicians all use scapegoats because they help groups and systems stay insulated and protected. Some of you likely connect with the feeling of being scapegoated by others, which is real and painful. But for the sake of the spirit of Holy Week and honest reflection, I'd like us to center our energies on how we may use scapegoats to deflect our own pain.

We can blame the church, politicians, other people, our addictions, our past, God, and ourselves for things that aren't even our fault. We can blame a long list of people, things, circumstances, and situations that help us find some temporary relief for our suffering. But any relief that scapegoating brings is only temporary because the reality always remains. In every system, after someone is scapegoated, the same ugly, unhealthy stuff remains and intensifies. Years ago, I was part of scapegoating a teammate who had a painful departure from our team. I got caught up with the false narrative others told me and failed to see her humanness. A year later, I was the one who was scapegoated and lost my job too. A few months after we started The Refuge, she was willing to meet with me, and I was able to make amends. We were able to name together how scapegoating is deeply connected to power and is a false fix that allows us to avoid the true realities of complex situations. Part of this reflective season is acknowledging our scapegoats—*the things we blame and direct our anger toward so that we don't have to look at the deeper pain within.*

Scapegoating divides us and perpetuates violence against ourselves, others, and God. Jesus brings shalom, wholeness, integration. He offers a better way, a humble way, a vulnerable way.

Scapegoating is easier at first; but in the end, it leads to death. Humility is harder at first; but in the end, it leads to life.

How have you scapegoated others to avoid pain?

MAUNDY THURSDAY

Giving and Receiving

"A new command I give you: Love one another. As I have loved you, so you must love one another. By this everyone will know that you are my disciples, if you love one another."

—John 13:34–35 NIV

Many years ago, during an intensive training we hosted at The Refuge for advocates and people willing to journey with people in hard places, we did a foot washing. Yikes! It's a vulnerable act. It's not hard at all for me to wash someone else's feet. But to sit there and let someone else wash mine, whoa, deep breaths.

The power shift in this act is revolutionary.

We like to be in control, not the other way around. For most of us, it's way easier to give than receive. It's easy to be in the driver's seat, the place where we are somehow helping or loving someone else, the place where we get to offer our love, time, or resources on someone's behalf. While I love the influx of focus on faith communities becoming more "missional," it can be dangerous, too, when we focus only on what we can do *to* or *for* others and forget about the transformational practice of *with* that equalizes power.

Love goes two ways, and power differentials shift only when there's reciprocity. This twist in the story of Jesus washing the disciples' feet (unheard of for people of stature like religious leaders, who had servants to do their foot washings) and calling us to do the same reminded me of how much humility it requires to let someone else wash ours. To humble ourselves and let others' good in, too, to allow ourselves to be vulnerable enough to receive, to respect and to recognize how pride and control are huge barriers can be transforming.

If you're reading in order during this season, today is Maundy Thursday. In Latin, *maundy* (*mandatum*) means "command," reflecting the commands that Jesus gave his disciples in the upper room the night he was betrayed. Today, we consider how Jesus turned traditional hierarchy upside down by washing his disciples' feet, much to their resistance. I wonder what it stirs up in us about power? What if the greater sacrifice is to let someone else wash our feet, instead of us washing theirs? To receive love, instead of giving it? To be like the disciples, and let the least likely person in the room pass love on to us?

True community embodied with power with is about washing each other's feet, loving others, and letting others love us.

This day shifts power in the ways it needs to be shifted—illuminating the importance of not only giving but humbly receiving too.

How can you practice receiving instead of giving today?

GOOD FRIDAY

The Side of Love

"For God's power is God's love."

— Sean Gladding[5]

I didn't grow up honoring Good Friday; in fact, it wasn't until the life of The Refuge when we started having a simple and unplugged gathering to hold space for this somber observance that I embraced its significance. For many who are part of more liturgical systems, these holy days are embedded into spiritual practices.

For most of us, however, death, despair, agony are not our favorite topics.

No matter what state of mind or life circumstance you find yourself in on Good Friday today, it's a day we can't skip over, because when it comes to power, it exemplifies almost all that we've been engaging with this past season. The distance between the shouts of joy to calls to violence was painfully short in this week that illuminates a truth that travels across the generations of history: *when power is threatened, look out.* When structures and beliefs and systems are challenged, look out. When religious leaders are confronted, look out. When calls for equity and inclusion are amplified, look out.

The story of entrenched power seems to remain timeless, and the current climate we are living in now, two millennia later, is much the same.

It makes me think of this Good Friday reflection from Cheryl Lawrie, whose work as a contemplative curator and prison chaplain in Australia is soul-stirring. I'm grateful she offered to freely share it with us. As you read this simple yet packed-with-beauty piece several times slowly, notice which words, phrases, or ideas might resonate with you right now, especially in light of everything we've been processing about power.

God, Who Are You?
by Cheryl Lawrie

What was it about Jesus
that was so confusing for governments
and for ordinary people?

Pilate couldn't make sense of Jesus
and half the time we can't either.

We want a God who comes in might and power to take all
    before him
and yet we get Jesus:
unmistakably human and vulnerable,
trouble-maker
peace-lover,
political subversive
always on the side of love, not power
human, even to the point of death.

We keep asking the question,
'God, who are you?'
in the hope we'll get a different answer.
And God just keeps coming back with this one.[6]

What is a word or phrase you can take
with you this Good Friday?

HOLY SATURDAY

The Now and the Not Yet

"In darkness we wait."

—The Refuge[7]

Yesterday, Good Friday, was packed with the drama of mobs and cross-carrying women weeping, Romans mocking, thieves crying out, and Jesus dying, his body being carried away. Now, we wake up to Holy Saturday, the day that is one of the most important days we can hold not only in the Easter story but also in the stories unfolding in our own relationship with shifting power and making collective change, together.

While Friday is about shock and being shocked, Holy Saturday is about reality setting in and the magnitude and thickness of grief. Today I hope we can hold on to lament in a different way than before—as a day that reminds us of how much is unhealed related to power in our culture today, and how painful that reality is.

While we are, indeed, making progress, right now we also see in the United States and abroad deep resistance against equity, diversity, and inclusion—in schools, faith, and government. We see unequal power being perpetuated and cemented into law where legal rights for LGBTQ+, women's reproductive choices, racial equity, and the ability to vote are going backward, not forward.

Today is a day that isn't mentioned in Scripture, but I imagine the disciples and Jesus' other followers stumbled aimlessly, feeling the shock of what just happened the day before. *Is this for real? How can this be so? How did all we hoped for come to this?*

For those of us who are passionate about disrupting power in the circles we live, move, and worship in, this discouragement and disbelief resonate currently with the crestfallen frustration of these questions: *Is this really where we still are, despite all our efforts? Is any of our work worth it? How has the political climate become this toxic? How can we ever come back from this much division and hate? Is healthy power even possible?*

We believe so passionately in *what could be* and yet we live in the *now and the not yet.*

That's what Holy Saturday can help us with.

We often don't see the fruits of our labor. We plant seeds we aren't sure will ever grow. We work hard on projects, programs, and possibilities that might not come to fruition for many years. We add our ripples to the mix not knowing where they will land. We labor in ways that sometimes may feel futile.

It helps to remember that no matter how committed we may be to the actions and practices we passionately believe in, we may not see the fruit. I'm always reminded of multiple biblical characters in both the Old and New Testaments who were courageous on the part of their conviction in following God yet died before they experienced the results of their work.

Part of our privilege—and our addiction to power—is that we want to have everything now. We want clear outcomes from our work. We often have a mindset of "if we do these certain things, we will get these results"; but that's now how it works as people of faith, as activists, as advocates, and as healers.

We often live in the not yet.

We hold on, not knowing the end of the story.

That's Holy Saturday.

What are some of the not yets you're holding this Holy Saturday?

Easter Sunday

EMBODY

"Easter us . . ."

—Walter Bruggemann[1]

From the crowds calling for crucifixion to the denials of following Jesus to the last words of "It is finished" to the sky darkened and all hope lost, Easter morning breaks through—resurrection, new life, a different kind of power that is unexplainable, makes no sense, confounds many, that is under the radar, appearing in strange interactions in small pockets of followers huddled together in fear and on the shorelines of the water, and while walking along the road.

A different kind of power. An Easter-ing, resurrecting power.

I love some of these other words for *resurrecting*: *awakening, bouncing back, breathing new life into, brightening, coming to life, making whole, overcoming, reawakening, recovering, rekindling, renewing, renovating, restoring, resuscitating, snapping out of it, springing up, strengthening.*

To stay the course on embodying our faith, our passion, our hope for the world, we need to be resurrected, Eastered.

As we honor this day, this place in our journey together, I love these simple words from a beautiful longer poem by Walter Brueggemann called "Easter Us." He writes,

    Easter us.
      salve wounds,

      break injustice,
      bring peace,
      . . . .
    Easter us in joy and strength."

The final line says—"Hear our thankful, grateful, unashamed Hallelujah!"[2]

When we think of the realities of power in our world, the inequities, discrimination, and oppression that is so contrary to the society we long for, it's sometimes hard to share a "thankful, grateful, unashamed Hallelujah!" I want to be there, but sometimes all we have is what Leonard Cohen sings—"it's a cold and it's a broken Hallelujah."[3] In our present reality of wars where tens of thousands of children are killed, brutal political divides, rising anti-Semitism and Islamophobia, mass shootings, the lack of affordable housing, our climate tipping into chaos, a culture of loneliness and division, and people at the top of the power structures making billions of dollars a day, keeping hope and seeing possibility require help beyond ourselves. Easter reminds us that we need help beyond ourselves and that there's room for all of it—the doubt, the joy, the fear, the peace, the reality, the possibility.

Today, I hope that we can honor our thankful, grateful, unashamed hallelujahs alongside our cold and broken ones. That we can acknowledge situations and circumstances celebrating resurrection, new life, possibility, and hope when it comes to shifting power and honor the smallest of movements that may seem insignificant on the surface, even futile. They are sweet embers of healing that we need to tend to.

This season may we commit our lives to being Eastered, to Eastering, to being resurrected, to resurrecting. These are verbs—active, ongoing, not an event but a way of living. Many of us are resurrecting in unique, wonderful, and scary ways when it comes to power. We're waking up to the truth about power. We're healing from abuse of power. We're breathing new life and possibilities into the systems and groups we're part of. We're recovering the ways of Jesus that have been buried underneath oppressive systems built on his name. We're making broken things more whole. We're reawakening to our responsibility to create more equitable systems that liberate, heal, and empower. We're renewing our commitment to embody something different in this broken, divided, and unjust world.

Resurrection is not born out of ease, comfort, and the status quo. It comes out of death, trouble, discomfort, dissonance. But the Easter story reminds us that it's always coming—again, again, again, and again. Lovely signs of hope, joy, peace, love, mercy, forgiveness, grace, justice, beauty, and a new kind of power.

Power with, not over or under.

Power that heals.

Power that's shared.

Power that equalizes and includes.

Power that creates and inspires.

Power that heals and repairs.

Power that restores dignity where it's been lost.

Power that tells the truth.

Power that disrupts.

Power that breaks injustice and brings peace.

Power that makes our broken world more whole.

How can you embody this kind of Easter power in brave new ways?

HOLY WEEK AND EASTER

Pause and Ponder: What Was Illuminated That We Can Embody?

Hopefully, looking at Jesus' days from Palm Sunday to Easter Sunday from a few eclectic and nontraditional angles illuminated something that maybe we hadn't considered before or can now frame in a new way. In these brief daily reflections, we can't encapsulate all the multilayered interactions Jesus had over the course of the week, but I hope it shined light on some particular thought, idea, reality, or example in our own life, leadership, and experience that we can take with us into the upcoming season of our story. Even just one thing to carry with us is enough.

For me, it's strength and courage to honor the now and the not yet when it comes to working on shifting power and avoiding the desire to see results the way I want or wish for. It helps me stay the course and remember the words of Reverend Dr. Martin Luther King Jr.: "The arc of the moral universe is long, but it bends toward justice."[4] That's often so hard to remember! Honoring the subversive ways of Jesus and the faithful activists and agitators who stir the pot, disrupt oppressive systems, and embody hope despite the obstacles inspire and challenge me to stay the course and keep this important truth front and center—*it's our role to keep turning over tables and disrupting power.* The more we're aware of power and its dynamics at work in ourselves, our relationships, groups, and systems, the better off we'll be. The more we are empowered to embody it in healthy, brave, and creative ways, the better off others will be. The more we work to cultivate more equitable power in the places where we live, work, and worship, the better off our world will be.

When it comes to power, what was illuminated
for you this season that you can embody more intentionally?

Wrestle, Reflect, Engage

Reflection Questions

1. What does disrupting power mean to you in your context? What part can you play embodying change in the groups and systems you are part of?
2. Where in your life have you found yourself caught in a subtle or overt connection to following a powerful leader? What impact did that have on you, your faith, your story?
3. What are some tables you want to turn over right now? Injustices you want to see made right, that make you want to scream, yell, and call out?
4. Consider the idea of scapegoating and how you may have scapegoated others in some way, shape, or form. Or maybe how you've been scapegoated? What can you learn from those painful situations about power?
5. How do you connect with the reality of it being easier to give than receive? What could receiving look like for you?
6. What are some ways you want to embody *Easter and resurrection* in this next season in the circles you are in? Think actions, not words.

Prompts for Grief and Gratitude

~ I lament the ways I have followed (*people, places, things*) _____.

~ I am deeply troubled by these injustices in the world, church, and my community or neighborhood: _____.

~ God, I am thankful for illumination of these truths, realities, and learning during this past season: _____.

Actions and Practices

1. Take time to review these past weeks together. What are some takeaways? What do you want to move into action in small or big ways? Write them down somewhere. Say them out loud to someone else. Find a way to acknowledge and honor them.
2. Consider enrolling in one of the Right Use of Power Institute's courses (rightuseofpower.org) if you haven't taken them before. Several are free, and it's a great way to continue to engage with healthy power.
3. Use your power to help shift something in the systems you are in. Take a concrete and tangible step (no matter how small) that you believe will catalyze change in your group or organization. Ask for support or accountability that will help you make these brave steps happen.

God,
help us more boldly create a more equitable future,
catalyzed by collaborative power, collective power, healthy power.
May we stay open, awake,
willing to practice new things that change old ways.
Keep challenging us to disrupt power in ways
that lead to life and liberation for all of us,
and courage to turn over tables that need turning.
Amen.

Conclusion

SUSTAIN

As we close our time together, let's take a big exhale. That was a lot to process, consider, and honor in all our different ways. When we started, I shared that this material is meant to be used in our unique contexts, realities, and stories and that we hopefully move what we are learning into action. The "right use of power" is lifelong work. Change never comes in a rush, and it always comes from a flow of energy from several directions.

Personal transformation is important, and that's where a lot of this journey has been focused during the season of Lent; however, personal work isn't enough.

Embodied actions, collectively, are what change things.

Shifting power will require all of us working in our different and unique ways to bring about change in our families, groups, workplaces, communities, churches, and the world. We need more bold advocates, vocal agitators, prophetic leaders, patient educators, and faithful practitioners to break down disparate power and reorder structures, systems, and frameworks toward greater equity. We need more humble learners and brave people across the spectrum of life who are willing to honestly examine our place in the story of power.

One of the most crucial ingredients we need is consistency and staying the course over the long haul. This, again, is something we can learn from recovery circles that embody healthy power through their framework and practices, always focusing on rightsizing ourselves. People in recovery don't just go for a while: they keep showing up, learning, growing, transforming, and supporting others in their journeys, too, for the rest of their lives. I've seen so much burst-of-energy work happen for a short period of time after there's some kind of racial crisis or world event. Then we slip back toward what is most safe and comfortable for the dominant power system, and no lasting progress is made.

Work on fostering more equal and healthy power is done over the slow, long story of advocacy and action, which I truly believe the world needs more of. When I was at the Southern Poverty Law Center in Montgomery, Alabama, I saw a sign that said, "Actions speak louder than posts." Actions speak louder than words, social media posts, Bible verses, and theological and spiritual platitudes.

And actions will truly shift power.

As we look back on all the various textures of power we explored together, it's time to bring some of these ideas and practices into the next chapter of our stories and consider what shifting and disrupting power looks like personally and in the systems we're part of. Where do we need to step up? Where do we need to step back? Who do we need to follow, and how do we need to lead differently? How can we share more? How can we not just listen better but truly do things differently?

Transformation looks different for all of us, but hopefully we can all be part of a collective, liberating power that frees, expands, multiplies, challenges, and heals.

For me, that's Easter hope.

A Word for Leaders

For those of you who lead faith communities or organizations of any type, I want to create some brief space to acknowledge how crucial your role is in catalyzing change. I believe this is why Jesus was often talking to the religious leaders—he knew that they were the ones who needed it the most. We all have blind spots. We all have areas we can work on to become healthier, more empowering leaders. We need to be so careful about the materials and leaders we are using and following. If we're in networks that promote typical hierarchical power, ascent theology, and a goal of always being bigger and better, then be careful. This kind of culture is not what is needed for a more free and expansive future for all people. Recognize the crucial role that you play in shifting power, and recognize that change requires hard work and different practices over a long period of time; however, those who hold power have the greatest ability to change it.

Listen for God's stirring in your heart: what might God be calling you to change, let go of, share, reconfigure, reconsider? Who can help support us in cultivating healthy community and in illuminating our blind spots? How can we be a part of networks that are dedicated to making new wineskins, not just new wine? I continue to learn how crucial it is to expand our circles beyond our norms and learn from business, nonprofit, and other industry leaders whose best practices have much to teach us. Most of all, find ways to gather those who are usually least listened to, whose voices are rarely heard, and whose stories are most often not told and learn from them.

Other tangible practices to consider:

- Acknowledge the power you hold in your role and name it more clearly in conversations and teams.
- Follow the lead of people in your organization who are typically on the underside of power—not just asking them for input but actually submitting yourself to their leadership publicly.
- Find or hire outside mentors, guides, or leaders with experience in changing systems to help you consider structural and cultural changes that create more equitable power.
- Practice sharing and giving away power—giving others the microphone, stepping back, and encouraging others to step up.
- Defend changes with critics who want to protect power.

Remember, we're not alone. While dismantling power and cultivating greater equity and health is not popular, there are plenty of people working hard to play a part in change. My hope is always that we'll find others in our organizations, cities, denominations, and regions and help sustain one another. My heart and prayer for all of us as leaders is simple.

May we embody . . .
less fear, less hierarchy, less control,
more humility, more sharing, more creativity,
eyes to see,
courage to act,
vulnerability to practice,
power that looks like loaves and fishes.
Amen.

Notes

Introduction: ENTER

1. Jim Henderson, "Off the Map Workshop with Richard Twiss" (workshop, Overlake Christian Church, Seattle, WA, November 2007).

2. Martin Luther King Jr., *The Radical King*, King Legacy, book 11, ed. Cornel West (Boston: Beacon Press, 2015), chap. 16, Kindle.

3. Cedar Barstow, "What's in Our Name?" Right Use of Power Institute, April 5, 2024, https://rightuseofpower.org/whats-in-our-name-by-dr-cedar -barstow/.

4. Cedar Barstow and Amanda Aguilera, "Types of Power," Intro to Right Use of Power Online Course, Right Use of Power Institute, July 29, 2021, https://rightuseofpower.org/courses/intro-to-right-use-of-power/.

5. Brené Brown, "Brené Brown on Power and Leadership," https:// brenebrown.com/resources/brene-brown-on-power-and-leadership/.

6. Henri J. M. Nouwen, *In the Name of Jesus: Reflections on Christian Leadership* (New York: Crossroad Publishing Co., 1989), 77.

The First Days of Lent: OPEN

1. Henri J. M. Nouwen, *The Inner Voice of Love: A Journey through Anguish to Freedom* (New York: Image Books, 1998), 78.

2. Thomas Keating, *Awakenings* (Chestnut Ridge, NY: Crossroad Publishing Co., 1998), 4.

3. Cedar Barstow, "What's in Our Name?" Right Use of Power Institute, April 5, 2024, https://rightuseofpower.org/whats-in-our-name-by-dr-cedar -barstow/.

4. Sasha Davis, "LGBTQIA+ Listen and Learn" (The Refuge, Broom-field, CO, July 23, 2023).

Week One: REVEAL

1. Indigenous Values Initiative, "Dum Diversas," Doctrine of Discovery Project (July 23, 2018), https://doctrineofdiscovery.org/dum-diversas/.

2. Richard Rohr, *Breathing Underwater* (Cincinnati: Franciscan Media, 2021), introduction, Kindle.

3. Rohr, introduction.

4. James Baldwin, "As Much Truth as One Can Bear," *New York Times*, January 14, 1962, https://timesmachine.nytimes.com/timesmachine /1962/01/14/118438007.html?pageNumber=120.

5. Heather McGhee, *The Sum of Us: What Racism Costs Everyone and How We Can Prosper Together* (New York; One World, 2021), 230.

6. Jane Coaston, "The Intersectionality Wars," *Vox*, May 28, 2019, https://www.vox.com/the-highlight/2019/5/20/18542843/intersec tionality-conservatism-law-race-gender-discrimination.

7. Columbia Law School, "Kimberlé Crenshaw on Intersectionality, More Than Two Decades Later," interview with Kimberlé Crenshaw, June 8, 2017, https://www.law.columbia.edu/news/archive/kimberle -crenshaw-intersectionality-more-two-decades-later.

8. Peggy McIntosh, "White Privilege and Male Privilege: A Personal Account of Coming to See Correspondences through Work in Women's Studies" (Working Paper 189, Wellesley Centers for Women, Wellesley, MA, 1988), https://nationalseedproject.org/Key-SEED-Texts/white -privilege-and-male-privilege.

9. Peggy McIntosh, "White Privilege: Unpacking the Invisible Knapsack," 1989, https://nationalseedproject.org/key-seed-texts/white -privilege-unpacking-the-invisible-knapsack.

10. Tears for Fears, "Everybody Wants to Rule the World," track 3 on *Songs from the Big Chair*, Virgin Music, 1985, LP.

11. Melvin Bray, "The 12 Steps and Co-creating Antiracist Community," The Refuge on Zoom, August 11, 2020.

12. Bray, "The 12 Steps and Co-creating Antiracist Community."

13. Melvin Bray, "Unlearn Inequity: Truth and Transformation Model," Collabyrinth, https://collabyrinthconsulting.com/unlearn-inequity/12-step -truth-transformation-model/.

14. Rachel Held Evans, "Patriarchy Doesn't 'Protect' Women: A response to John Piper," March 20, 2018, https://rachelheldevans.com /blog/me-too-john-piper.

Week Two: LAMENT

1. Cole Arthur Riley, *This Here Flesh: Spirituality, Liberation, and the Stories That Make Us* (New York: Convergent Books, 2022), chap. 8, Kindle.

2. Bizzy Feekes, "Lament in 2020," Faithward, https://www.faithward.org/lament-in-2020/.

3. Resmaa Menakem, *My Grandmother's Hands: Racialized Trauma and the Pathway to Mending Our Hearts and Bodies* (Las Vegas: Central Recovery Press, 2017), chap. 1, Kindle.

4. Roger C., *The Little Book: A Collection of Alternative 12 Steps* (Bethesda, MD: AA Agnostica, 2020).

5. Katie Asmus, personal conversation, unpublished statement.

6. Myisha T. Hall, *Heal Your Way Forward: The Co-conspirator's Guide to an Antiracist Future* (New Egypt, NJ: Row House Publishing, 2022), chap. 5, Kindle.

7. Austin Channing Brown, *I'm Still Here: Black Dignity in a World Made for Whiteness* (New York: Convergence Books, 2018), chap. 14, Kindle.

8. Joan Podrazik, "Maya Angelou's Lesson for Oprah," Huffpost.com, January 16, 2013, https://www.huffpost.com/entry/maya-angelou-oprah-winfrey_n_2372128.

9. Elizabeth Perry, "Intent versus Impact: A Formula for Better Communication," BetterUp, July 14, 2021, https://www.betterup.com/blog/intent-vs-impact.

Week 3: REPENT

1. "The Hebrew Meaning of Shabbat Teshuvah," Hebrewversity, https://www.hebrewversity.com/hebrew-meaning-shabbat-teshuvah/.

2. Thich Nhat Hanh, *Fear: Essential Wisdom for Getting through the Storm* (New York: HarperOne, 2012), chap. 6, Kindle.

3. Lilla Watson, "Let Us Work Together," Uniting Church in Australia, https://uniting.church/lilla-watson-let-us-work-together/.

4. Jared Escobar, "Be Comfortable Being Uncomfortable," in *Wild, Beautiful, Free* (Arvada, CO: Boss, 2020), epilogue.

5. Howard Thurman, *Jesus and the Disinherited* (Boston: Beacon Press, 2012), chap. 1, Kindle.

6. Bryan Stevenson, *Just Mercy: A Story of Justice and Redemption* (New York: Random House, 2014), introduction, Kindle.

Week 4: DISRUPT

1. Bennito L. Kelty, "Activist Angela Davis Urges Cooperation against Injustice," *Columbia Missourian*, January 24, 2017, https://www.columbiamissourian.com/news/local/activist-angela-davis-urges-cooperation-against-injustice/article_f77a21a0-e2b0-11e6-9d29-130699fe9e6d.html.

2. "Heretics," Vocal Bank Blog, February 22, 2017, https://vocabbankblog.wordpress.com/2017/02/22/heretics/.

3. Melvin Bray, "Equity Is a Practice" (virtual workshop, The Refuge, Broomfield, CO, January 8, 2024).

4. Bray, "Equity Is a Practice."

5. bell hooks, *All about Love: New Visions* (New York: William Morrow, 2018), chap. 3, Kindle.

6. Brené Brown (@BreneBrown), "Courage is a heart word. Be brave. Love hard," Twitter Photo, February 14, 2018, https://x.com/BreneBrown/status/963793534817009664?lang=en.

7. Brené Brown, *The Gifts of Imperfection: Let Go of Who You Think You're Supposed to Be and Embrace Who You Are* (Center City, MN: Hazelden, 2010), 12.

8. Brown, *The Gifts of Imperfection*, 12–13.

9. Idelette McVicker, *Recovering Racists: Dismantling White Supremacy and Reclaiming Our Humanity* (Ada, MI: Brazos Press, 2022), 84–85.

10. Mirabai Starr, *Wild Mercy: Living the Fierce and Tender Wisdom of the Women Mystics* (Boulder, CO: Sounds True, 2019), chap. 5, Kindle.

11. Eva Rodriguez, "Bryan Stevenson Savors Victory in Supreme Court Ruling on Juvenile Life Sentences," *The Washington Post*, June 25, 2012, https://www.washingtonpost.com/lifestyle/style/bryan-stevenson-savors-victory-in-supreme-court-ruling-on-juvenile-life-sentences/2012/06/25/gJQA8Wqm2V_story.html.

12. *John Lewis: Good Trouble*, directed by Dawn Porter (Hollywood, CA: AGC Studios, 2020).

13. Bray, "Equity Is a Practice."

Week Five: CULTIVATE

1. Resmaa Menakem, *My Grandmother's Hands: Racialized Trauma and the Pathway to Mending Our Hearts and Bodies* (Las Vegas: Central Recovery Press, 2017), chap 1, Kindle.

2. Kaitlin B. Curtis, *Native: Identity, Belonging, and Discovering God* (Grand Rapids, MI: Brazos Press, 2020), 16.

3. Brené Brown, "Brené Brown on Power and Leadership," https://brenebrown.com/resources/brene-brown-on-power-and-leadership.

4. Robin Wall Kimmerer, *Braiding Sweetgrass: Indigenous Wisdom, Scientific Knowledge, and the Teaching of Plants* (Minneapolis: Milkweed Editions, 2013), chap. 22, Kindle.

5. Kimmerer, chap. 13.

6. Valarie Kaur, *See No Stranger: A Memoir and Manifesto of Revolutionary Love* (New York: One World, 2022), xvii.

7. "Shalom," *Strong's Exhaustive Concordance*, 7965, Bible Hub, https://biblehub.com/hebrew/7965.htm.

8. Pam Wilhelms Johnston, "Soul of the Next Economy Theology Camp" (The Refuge, Denver Community Church, Denver, CO, September 2013).

9. Johnston, "Soul of the Next Economy Theology Camp."

10. Elizabeth Gilbert, *Big Magic: Creative Living beyond Fear* (New York: Riverhead Books, 2015), part 4, Kindle.

11. Walter Brueggemann, *The Prophetic Imagination: 40th Anniversary Edition* (Minneapolis: Fortress Press), 23.

12. Brown, "Brené Brown on Power and Leadership."

Holy Week: ILLUMINATE

1. Jeff Jernigan, "Anger Can Be Our Friend," *Contentment*, Spring 2022, 44.

2. Martin Luther King Jr., "A Letter from Birmingham Jail," https://learning.hccs.edu/faculty/emily.klotz/engl1302-7/course-readings/a-letter-from-birmingham-jail-martin-luther-king-jr/view.

3. Dictionary.com, s.v. "Scapegoat," accessed August 8, 2024, https://www.dictionary.com/browse/scapegoat.

4. Bernard Keenan, "Mimetic Desire and the Scapegoat: Notes on the Thought of René Girard," CLT, September 4, 2023, https://criticallegalthinking.com/2023/09/04/mimetic-desire-the-scapegoat-notes-on-the-thought-of-rene-girard/.

5. Sean Gladding, *The Story of God, the Story of Us* (Downers Grove, IL: InterVarsity Press, 2010), 192.

6. Cheryl Lawrie, "Good Friday Reflection: God Who Are You?" re-worship.blogspot.com, https://re-worship.blogspot.com/2018/03/good-friday-reflection-god-who-are-you.html.

7. The Refuge @therefugeco, "In Darkness We Wait" Facebook, April 8, 2023, Facebook.com/therefugecolorado.

Easter Sunday: EMBODY

1. Walter Brueggemann, "Easter Us," in *Awed to Heaven, Rooted in Earth: Prayers of Walter Brueggemann* (Minneapolis: Fortress Press, 2003), chap. 9, Kindle.

2. Brueggemann, "Easter Us."

3. Leonard Cohen, "Hallelujah," track 5 on *Various Positions*, 1984, Columbia Records.

4. Martin Luther King Jr., *The Radical King,* King Legacy, book 11, ed. Cornel West (Boston: Beacon Press, 2015), chap. 16, Kindle.

Recommended Resources

Right Use of Power Institute, https://rightuseofpower.org.
Unlearning Inequity with Melvin Bray, https://collabyrinthconsulting.com
/unlearn-inequity.
Brené Brown on Power and Leadership, https://brenebrown.com/resources
/brene-brown-on-power-and-leadership/.
Real Power: Stages of Power in Organizations, Janet O. Hagberg (Salem, WI:
Sheffield Publishing, 2002).
The Web of Inclusion: Architecture for Building Great Organizations, Sally
Helgesen (Santa Ana, CA: Beard Publishing, 2005).
*Unsettling Truths: The Ongoing, Dehumanizing Legacy of the Doctrine
of Discovery*, Mark Charles and Soong-Chan Rah (Downers Grove,
IL: InterVarsity, 2019).

www.ingramcontent.com/pod-product-compliance
Ingram Content Group UK Ltd.
Pitfield, Milton Keynes, MK11 3LW, UK
UKHW021439120225
4561UKWH00035B/917

9 780664 268312